Patriarchal Attitudes

PATRIARCHAL ATTITUDES

Women in Society

EVA FIGES

Persea Books

New York

First published in Great Britain in 1970 by Faber and Faber,
and by Virago, Ltd. in 1978. Republished by Macmillan
Educational Ltd. in 1986. First published in the United
States of America by Stein & Day in 1970. First Persea
edition published in 1987.

For information, address the publisher:

Persea Books
225 Lafayette Street
New York, New York 10012

Library of Congress Cataloging-in-Publication Data

Figes, Eva.
    Patriarchal attitudes.

    Reprint. Previously published: New York: Stein and Day,
1970. With new introd.
    Bibliography: p.
    Includes index.
    1. Women—History. 2. Sex role. 3. Feminism.
I. Title
HQ1121.F53   1987   305.4′2   87-2379
ISBN 0-89255-122-4 (pbk.)

Manufactured in the United States of America
First printing

Contents

Introduction

This book first appeared in 1970, a few months before Germaine Greer's *The Female Eunuch* and Kate Millett's *Sexual Politics*. The intellectual atmosphere in which the book was produced is a measure of the progress its ideas have made since then, for I remember that any mention of the work I was engaged in would lead to stormy arguments between husbands and wives round the dinner table. Men told me I was making a mistake, a publisher suggested I had a 'chip on my shoulder', someone else warned me that I would never change men's minds, and I answered that I did not need to: it was enough to change women.

It turned out that I was right, and I count myself lucky to have written the right book at the right moment. I always knew from my reading that other people (including distinugished men) had said much the same thing as I was saying, but in 1970 it became clear that feminism was an idea whose moment had come. Within months the publisher who had accused me of having a chip on my shoulder announced himself proud to be publishing the book, and to be 'associated with the movement'. All men of good will and reasonable education paid lip service, at least, to the new philosophy of sexual equality, and male authority embarked on a process of back-tracking. Freudian psycho-analysts cried *mea culpa* and admitted their error, theories of male aggression as a form of creativity quietly disappeared from bookshelves, and Dr Spock suddenly noticed that the children of working mothers were more self-reliant and a good deal nicer to have around the home.

Introduction

It seemed too good to be true, and in many ways it was. With hindsight, it proved much easier to change public opinion than to change the inequalities built into the fabric of society. However, public opinion is a necessary first friend in bringing change about, and at least sexual inequality ceased to be regarded as normal and even desirable for the good of society as a whole. At long last the major political parties had to take the women's vote seriously, and in 1975 the Sex Discrimination Act was passed, after several private members' bills had been thrown out by the House of Commons. The Act, like the Equal Opportunities Commission, may have accomplished far too little in real terms, but at least the aspirations of women are publicly recognised as just.

So how much, and how little, has changed since 1970? In areas, particularly those governing personal relationships between men and women, there have been very big changes. Marriage is no longer the economic trap (nor the cosy meal ticket) that it once was for women. We have got used to the working wife, the house husband, the single parent, and even the couple who do not marry at all. Abortion is now widely accepted in this country, and is beginning to be accepted in countries where state religion once made it an impossibility. Divorce settlements now take into account the contribution made by the woman who stays at home to raise children, but also recognise that an ex-husband's liability should be limited.

The image of women projected by the mass media has also changed radically. For better or worse, we have had a woman prime minister for several years, who is nothing if not authoritative, and who knows how to use the media to her advantage. She may be detestable, but she is indubitably in charge. In 1970 it was unheard of for a woman to read the news on television, give the weather forecast, or present programmes on current affairs. All this may seem little more than cosmetics, but it is more. Women are now making important programmes, not just presenting them. And it is now possible to conceive of a female prime minister without first murdering the language by referring to 'the prime ministress'.

Perhaps most hopefully, a whole generation of young women

7

has grown up since 1970 whose attitudes and expectations have been strongly influenced by the feminism that swept through the Western world about that time. They are independent, self-reliant, and take the initiative in ending unsatisfactory marriages, as recent statistics show.

On the negative side, much in the fabric of our society has not changed, and a lot more has changed for the worse, a situation which inevitably affects the aspirations of women. The gap between male and female earnings, both in Britain and the rest of the world, is as wide as ever. Women work the longest hours and own the least property. The proportion of women members in the House of Commons is as low as ever, and our first woman prime minister is hostile to feminism and does not have a single woman in her Cabinet.

At a bleaker level, mass unemployment, economic recession and a resurgence of *laissez-faire* Toryism have made many aspirations voiced in this book and elsewhere fifteen years ago an impossibility. In particular, the dream of proper family support, crèches for working mothers and universal nursery education as a crucial factor for radical social change have become a total impossibility within the foreseeable future. It is partly for this reason that feminism today seems to have lost its way, and to lack clear objectives.

There are of course many issues to which women can and should address themselves. The moral storms about abortion may have largely died away, but there are other issues concerning women's control over their own bodies which are still contentious, including methods of birth control, infertility, surrogate motherhood, the menopause, and the treatment of women during childbirth. Attitudes to rape are also being changed by feminists, and certain types of pornography are being challenged as an unacceptable use and abuse of women. And in the anti-nuclear peace movement, women's courage and tenacity has won the admiration of all who fear for the very future of mankind.

So the gains and losses in the struggle seem about equally balanced, and the losses affect more than just women. For many people it is a bad time to be alive, and to be young is very hell.

Introduction

The New Jerusalem may seem a lot further away than it did in 1970, but mankind has always been remarkably resilient in the face of unmitigated disaster, and womankind has certainly shown herself to be so.

Eva Figes, 1986

To begin with . . .

. . . it was intended that this should be a book about women in relation to society as a whole, on the traditional role they have played for so long, the reasons for it, and the ways that I think this role should now change. It has turned out to be a book largely about men. Very early on in my researches I realized that this was going to be inevitable, as soon as I found that I would get no clear or convincing answer to one fundamental question. I am referring to the vexed question of secondary sexual differences with regard to behaviour, ability, and so on.

We all know about the primary differences, and most of us tend to assume that when human beings have such different physical functions their mental functioning must also differ radically. The differing social behaviour of men and women now and in the past would tend to confirm this assumption, but it is only an assumption, and so far scientific research has either been highly inconclusive or has tended to point in the other direction: in favour of nurture rather than nature.

We know that women live longer, that they are less vulnerable to disease for genetic reasons, and that men are usually stronger and more muscular, though it is possible that this state of affairs has evolved as a result of a sexual division of work. Muscles have to be used in order to develop. Margaret Mead discovered that the males of Bali did little heavy work and were as slight as their womenfolk, but that the Balinese men who worked as dock coolies under European supervision developed the heavy musculature which we associate with men.[1]

[1] Margaret Mead, *Sex and Temperament in Three Primitive Societies*.

To begin with . . .

There is a good deal of vague talk about sex hormones nowadays, but in fact we know almost nothing about the link between these hormones and behaviour, although we know that the hormone levels do affect specifically sexual behaviour. I suppose there is a case for saying that specifically sexual behaviour will also be more general behaviour. For instance, we know that there is a systematic fluctuation of progesterone levels during the woman's menstrual cycle, and the levels vary considerably more during pregnancy. This could account for the fact that women tend to suffer from 'moods', are often mildly panic-depressive, and can have particularly severe depressions after childbirth. Similarly one could say that, since the male takes the initiative, male sexual arousal must inevitably be linked with aggression. Hormone experiments have been made with monkeys,[1] following on the finding that infant male monkeys are more aggressive than infant female monkeys. Pregnant monkeys were treated with testosterone, and as a result the experimenters succeeded in producing female offspring with pseudo-hermaphroditic features, and these females were more aggressive and engaged in more rough-and-tumble play. After three years the aggressive behaviour appeared to have diminished, and one possible interpretation of this experiment is that the pre-natal hormone level can condition very early behaviour long enough for social learning to take over, or that hormones can affect the whole life-span even after they are no longer present in the body.

This is an interesting idea, but rather far-fetched. The fact is that male and female hormone levels do not differ significantly before puberty, and yet by the age of four or five small boys behave very differently from small girls. One is forced to the conclusion that this behaviour has been largely learned, and this idea is borne out by studies of human beings who, because of ambiguous or hermaphroditic genital features, were assigned to the wrong sex at birth. These studies[2] suggested that gender role-playing was determined by environmental conditions, and that a

[1] *The Development of Sex Differences*, edited by Eleanor E. Maccoby (Tavistock Publications, 1967), p. 15.
[2] Ibid., pp. 15–17.

person would adjust to the 'wrong' sex label, but that there was a critical period of sexual identity fixing in early childhood. So, for instance, a girl could be wrongly reared as a boy without much trouble, but serious psychological difficulty would result if a small girl was required to 'become' a boy after the age of about three.

If there is almost no evidence in favour of nature there is over-whelming evidence in favour of nurture: we keep looking for the needle in the haystack and all the time the haystack is staring us in the face. Small boys and girls have a very clear idea of sexual role-playing in society and conform to that idea long before puberty, even before they have any real notion of genital differ-ences. Lawrence Kohlberg,[1] of Chicago University, whose tests on children suggested that modern enlightened parenthood made little difference on this point, concluded that 'the process of form-ing a constant gender identity is not a unique process determined by instinctual wishes and identifications, but a part of the general process of conceptual growth'. He rejects the Freudian theory of instincts and stresses that 'the child's sexual identity is maintained by a motivated adaption to physical-social reality and by the need to preserve a stable and positive self-image'. Whilst Walter Mischel[2] of Stanford University stresses that sexual conformity is linked with rewards, Kohlberg, I think rightly, emphasizes that direct rewards are not necessary for conformity, and that 'socially shared expectations' alone 'exert a normative force upon the individual'.

And what are these norms? We can talk about 'masculinity' and 'femininity' until the cows come home, but the fact is that all attempts at psychometrics only result, and can only result, in a reflection of society as it is at present; what is more, in studying masculine and feminine personality all that the psychometrist is doing is relating human beings to the norms that he himself has set up. And if people are reporting on themselves (and self-reports are much used in such studies) that is what they are doing too. Thus the psychologist tends to come up with the amazing dis-covery that original thinking, creativity and a high level of general intelligence are associated with more 'feminine' men and more

[1] Ibid., pp. 82 and following.   [2] Ibid., pp. 56 and following.

'masculine' women,[1] which he may try to explain in terms of 'bisexuality', when in fact the explanation is much more simple: by assigning sex roles and sex-related interests we limit human possibilities, but some people refuse to allow themselves to be repressed in such a fashion. When a woman is required to choose between marriage and a career it does of course amount to repression on a monstrous scale.

'I deny that any one knows, or can know, the nature of the two sexes, as long as they have only been seen in their present relation to one another,' wrote John Stuart Mill a hundred years ago, and modern psychology tends to confirm this view, whilst biology has little to offer to bolster all those old prejudices and assumptions. Most of the feminine traits that psychometrics have revealed can be easily explained in sociological terms. So woman is less dominant because that is what society requires of her, more emotional because her thoughts and education have been directed to the heart rather than the head, more conservative because hearth and home do not change much and do not (like the competitive world of business and public affairs) require the capacity for change as a condition for survival. Pioneers in this field had reached similar conclusions. Helen Thomson had written at the beginning of the century: 'The point to be emphasized as the outcome of this study is that, according to our present light, the psychological differences of sex seem to be largely due, not to difference of average capacity, nor to difference in type of mental activity, but to differences in the social influences brought to bear in the developing individual from early infancy to adult years',[2] and Terman and Miles,[3] writing thirty years later, in 1936, reached a similar conclusion.

Psychometric research seems able to do little beyond measuring the present state of affairs within a given society, and it also tends to measure by the standards set up by that society. One form of research which tries to remedy this by jumping outside its own society in place and time and examining other cultures, is anthro-

---

[1] Ibid., p. 35.
[2] Dr. Helen B. Thomson, *The Mental Traits of Sex* (1903); quoted by Viola Klein, *The Feminine Character*.
[3] Terman and Miles, *Sex and Personality: Studies in Masculinity and Femininity* (1936).

pology. On the vexed topic of the 'nature' of men and women the anthropologist has certain advantages. Psychologists work with the material to hand, the members or victims of their own society, and when they elaborate their findings into a more general theory the reader must be on his guard. Everyone has to work their way through the Oedipal situation, declares Freud. Pardon me, answers Malinowski, but in the place where I work families do not recognize the father figure, so the situation simply never arises in the first place. Exit Freud.

For this reason the evidence of anthropologists is particularly valuable for us. Margaret Mead, who specifically concerned herself with this problem, is emphatic: 'The evidence is overwhelmingly in favour of the strength of social conditioning' she wrote in *Sex and Temperament in Three Primitive Societies*. Other anthropologists stress the importance of social conditioning in human behaviour. 'Men do not act', wrote Claude Lévi-Strauss in *Totemism*, 'as members of a group, in accordance with what each feels as an individual; each man feels as a function of the way in which he is permitted or obliged to act. Customs are given as external norms before giving rise to internal sentiments, and these non-sentient norms determine the sentiments of individuals as well as the circumstances in which they may, or must, be displayed.' And Malinowski wrote in *Sex and Repression in Savage Society*: 'Education consists in the last instance in the building up of complex and artificial habit responses, of the organization of emotions into sentiments.'

The word 'artificial' begs the question: what is a 'natural' man or woman? One is forced to answer that there is no such thing, unless one concludes that, since man is a social animal, his 'natural' condition is to *be* artificially conditioned, with variations in time and place. For centuries the world 'nature' has been used to bolster prejudices or to express, not reality, but a state of affairs that the user would wish to see. This has been true of both poets and philosophers, moralists and theologians. Nowadays we have few illusions about our inglorious ancestry, but the fact still remains that we are *not* apes; when a man catches a train and sits in an office dictating letters and making telephone calls it has precious little relationship with hunting in a carnivorous pack. A woman rarely suckles her young, and compared to the primates she has much more sex and breeds but rarely—for most of her fertile years she is kept artificially infertile. We still talk vaguely about instincts, and of the maternal instinct in particular, and we tend to ascribe the discontents and dissatisfactions of our modern, everyday lives to the frustration of these supposed natural instincts. But if our behaviour were so profoundly instinctual we would all be much more disturbed—the man confined to an office all day would run amok, a woman treated with the pill for any length of time would be a mental case.

Notice that Malinowski and Lévi-Strauss were talking, not about conventions, not about moral codes and social customs, but about our *feelings*. This book will be largely concerned with external norms which give rise to internal sentiments, with the organization of emotions into sentiments. Our feelings on the love between men and women, on marriage and parenthood, on the family and on ourselves as fathers, wives and mothers, are largely conditioned by the society which produced us, more so than we realize. The types of women that our society has produced in the past, the roles they have played or failed to play, sprang from the dictates and expectations of men. Women have been largely man-made, and even today numerous psychological studies have revealed that women and girls are still more dependent on social approval than men. Which is why this book has turned out to be almost exclusively on the subject of men, on their attitudes towards women, because it is these attitudes that shaped us.

I think we are only just beginning to realize the enormous importance of environment, not only with regard to men and women, but with regard to one human being and another, and these, do not forget, will differ in character far more glaringly than any differentiation based on sex. The fact that one man will differ so markedly in character and abilities from another man should surely allow us to forget about hormones and menstrual cycles for a little while and concentrate on more obvious things. On the factor of expectation, for example, which is particularly important. Recent experiments have revealed that if a teacher was told that a group of children, selected at random, had exceptional ability and should make rapid progress, those children really did make remarkable progress, and after a time their I.Q. performance rose by thirty or forty points.[1] So far most women have lived down to the abysmally low standard socially expected of them. Even the modern female child is more easily discouraged by failure than a boy and has a low expectation of success in carrying out a given task.[2] And for the adult woman incentives as well as lack of high expectations pull the other way. Woman, presented with an image in a mirror, has danced to that image in a hypnotic trance. And because she thought the image was herself, it became just that.

I cannot do better than to reiterate the words of Havelock Ellis,[3] written half a century ago but still valid today:

> We have to recognise that our present knowledge of men and women cannot tell us what they might be or what they ought to be, but what they actually are, under the conditions of civilisation. By showing us that under varying conditions men and women are, within certain limits, indefinitely modifiable, a precise knowledge of the actual facts of the life of men and women forbids us to dogmatize rigidly concerning the respective spheres of men and women. . . . If this is not exactly the result which we set out to attain, it is still a result of very considerable importance.

A result of very considerable importance. Only blind obstinacy could make a person refuse to accept 'no answer' or at least 'not proven' as in itself an answer of a kind, the mindless obstinacy that goes with deeply rooted prejudices. Foolishly, I suppose, Ellis hoped that his book would at least help to clear away the 'thick undergrowth of prepossession and superstition which flourishes in the region . . . to a greater extent than in any other region'. It appears to have done nothing of the kind, and I suppose it would be too much to hope that my book will succeed where his failed. One can slash out at the undergrowth, but it has a way of growing up again overnight, whatever one does, or says.

[1] Rosenthal and Jacobson, *Pygmalion in the Classroom*, referred to by Liam Hudson in an article entitled 'Grey Matter', published in the *New Statesman* ,14th February 1969.
[2] *The Development of Sex Differences*, pp. 32–3.
[3] Havelock Ellis, *Man and Woman: A Study of Human Secondary Sexual Characters*.

I

A Man's World

The first thing that strikes one about the image in the mirror to which we dance is the fact that it was created by man; not by men and women jointly for common ends, not by women for themselves, but by men. One could say that this is the real difficulty: the fact that the mirror is distorted. Man's vision of woman is not objective, but an uneasy combination of what he wishes her to be and what he fears her to be, and it is to this mirror image that woman has had to comply. Man has also been required to live up to an image, but since it was made for him by his father it was more likely to fit in with his own desires: bravery could mean the courage to make straight for what you want. There is no conflict except the external rivalry between men who want the same things. It is only the man who is not sure about his wants, who questions the naked power and simple pleasures traditionally sought after and competed for, who becomes neurotic, a misfit Hamlet.

But woman is taught to desire not what her mother desired for herself, but what her father and all men find desirable in a woman. Not what she *is,* but should be. Man is a good deal more lenient with himself: he may say that men should be brave, unselfish, yet the fact that he is weak and egotistic is looked upon as a regrettable falling away from the ideal standard which is only to be expected in human beings. But since the standard of womanhood is set by men for men and not by women, no relaxation of standards is allowable, she is either an absolute woman or nothing at all, totally rejected. This is one of the reasons why the male image of woman has a tendency to split into two, into black and white, Virgin Mary and

17

Scarlet Woman, angel of mercy and prostitute, gentle companion and intolerable bluestocking. A rigid image must of necessity split, since the most compliant reality can hardly fit it absolutely. There are other reasons for this very noticeable split, for man's capacity for putting woman on a pedestal and at the same time trampling her underfoot, which will be examined in detail later.

It is reasonable to assume that when men talk about women or women about men a certain amount of bias must be inevitable. Of course. Men and women do have different standpoints, and it is only natural that they should speak from their own point of view. But this, oddly enough, is an obvious point which is never conceded. Thousands of books have been written about women, many studies have been made of them, many poems written, dozens of philosophical and psychological essays written. And in almost all cases the author has been a man. So consistently has the author been male that the point has been totally overlooked, taken for granted. Certainly the idea of bias is never entertained. But the moment a woman sets pen to paper it is another matter. I was accused of bias before I had even written a word of this book, simply on the grounds that I was a woman. I am not denying it, of course, but a man is just as unable to get out of his own skin. But because he denies the necessity to try and do so he is in fact more biased. George Eliot wrote that Sir James Cheetham, in *Middlemarch*, was not even aware that he was more stupid than Dorothea, the girl he was in love with, so that her cleverness did not worry him: 'A man's mind—what there is of it—has always the advantage of being masculine,—as the smallest birch-tree is of a higher kind than the most soaring palm,—and even his ignorance is of a sounder quality.' It is from this sounder ignorance that men tend to scoff at the new wave of articulate women, mostly writers, who have tried to understand the situation, if only from their own point of view. And arrogance on one side breeds stridency on the other.

Furthermore, it is not only one glass, but the whole hall of mirrors which is male-created. We are born into a world where the great discoverers, philosophers, artists and scientists have almost all been male. Male law-makers, male conquerors, even the God

18

perpetuated in tradition, who still somehow haunts the early days of childhood, is male. Our whole code of morality was formulated by men. Things are changing, of course, but the weight of tradition must lie heavy on not one, but several generations. If it were just a question of social codes the change would be slow enough, since social forms of behaviour do in fact change much more slowly than people like to imagine, and are naturally perpetuated through the family; but there is so much more to contend with—one might say that for the great majority of women the obvious course of events is to subside meekly or gracefully into the tradition role assigned to them, whilst for the really determined woman, for whom that role is inadequate, unsatisfactory or simply unavailable, there is an uphill struggle to compete in a game where all the rules have been laid down by the other party without her having been consulted, and where all the vital moves were probably made before she arrived on the scene.

Virginia Woolf[1] thought that one of the reasons why women had been so successful at writing novels was that this was a relatively new art form where all the rules had not been laid down. We find a similar explanation in one of her most eminent predecessors, George Eliot. In an essay entitled 'Silly Novels by Lady Novelists' she wrote: 'No educational restrictions can shut women out from the materials of fiction, and there is no species of art which is so free from rigid requirements. Like crystalline masses, it may take any form, and yet be beautiful.' (If Virginia Woolf ever came across that phrase about crystalline masses I think she would have felt a small thrill of recognition, just as I did.)

It is fairly obvious that women with a modicum of home education could compete in the field of novel writing, and that women would be automatically excluded from any art or science that required specialized training. But we are less conscious of the fact that the language which we use has itself been created, that we have mathematical systems, musical systems, that in thinking we use counters that have already been created for us and passed down by tradition. If we think of the great symphonies we hear the masculine chords of Beethoven, impossible to imagine a woman having

1 Virginia Woolf, *A Room of One's Own.*

written most of his music, or so we tend to assume. The piano sonatas were written for male fingers, I doubt if many women could cope with them physically, and perhaps not psychologically. If we think of the peak of achievement in another sphere than that of music, the visual arts for instance, we would find it hard to imagine a woman coping with the physical labour of the Sistine chapel ceiling, or conceiving a powerful figure like Moses in stone. And yet the work of a modern sculptress like Barbara Hepworth can be masculine enough. The existing idioms are probably only alien to women because we have been conditioned in our responses, to shun arduous physical labour and avoid certain images as unfeminine.

We are now in the realm of speculation, of course. Impossible to turn the clock back and run the experiment through again. Perhaps we could have a female Moses, the epitome of dignified matriarchy, and sweeping symphonies composed by women. Or would our eyes and ear be attuned to delicacy, subtle nuances, filigree textures?

But the realm of art is only one aspect of the way in which tradition is perpetuated. Of far more immediate importance is the body of ideas which is passed down through education from one generation to the next. Even when ideas are recognized by all or some to be out of date and superseded, they are still handed down as part of our heritage through education. For example, we are all familiar with some of the Bible stories, and most of us carry in our heads a kind of childhood world inhabited by Adam and Eve, Noah in his Ark, and three kings following a magic moving star to Bethlehem. It is a world which rational thinking rejects but which we still value: the fact that we do value it is proved in the way we make use of its imagery, perpetuate it in traditional rites, and give our children wooden arks for Christmas. We are also taught about the Pharaohs of Egypt, the Hanging Gardens of Babylon, and the fact that people used to think that the earth was flat, and that the sun and stars circulated round it. Almost nothing gets lost, in a sense part of us goes on knowing that three kings brought gifts, guided by a moving star, and every child can see that it is the sun moving across the sky and that ground is flat.

We think of ourselves as up to date, but our upbringing, like that of the great teachers and scientists and philosophers whom we absorb and allow to guide us, involves a body of learning which only changes its shape very slowly, where little gets lost and nothing is ever really thrown out totally. And of course we are still in a state of becoming. As Lévi-Strauss[1] pointed out, there is no fundamental difference in the way we think and the way a savage thinks. We guess, we assume, we construct false theories, moving forward in the only way possible, fumbling in the dark.

The fact that most of us take all this for granted, that we do not make the effort to stand aside and, in a sense, step outside of our own skins for a while and take a long, hard, questioning look, in itself helps to perpetuate tradition, means that we fit that much more easily into the role society assigns us, accepting the external norms. And no wonder: standing outside of oneself is a difficult process that rapidly makes one dizzy. No one can keep it up for long. But it is essential that we try, if we are to make the most of our lives and capacities in a changing world.

When it comes to the external norms that relate to the position of men and women in society, their relationship to the outside world and to each other, the male half of the population has had little enough motivation to stand aside and analyse the accepted body of opinion at any one time. By questioning it he has and had nothing to gain and everything to lose: he would lose not only social and economic advantages, but something far more precious, a sense of his own superiority which bolsters his ego both in his public and his private life. John Stuart Mill[2] explained the lack of change in this area convincingly by saying that when it came to political revolution against an autocracy only a privileged minority had something to gain by resisting the forces of change, but in changing the relationship of men to women every man, rich or poor, stood to lose by a change. And each woman stood to lose by an open challenge of her master's supremacy. But now, as a hundred years ago when Mill was writing, the fact that change should be slow in this area is taken as another proof of the idea that the existing order is the only natural or possible one.

[1] Claude Lévi-Strauss, *Totemism* and *The Savage Mind*.
[2] John Stuart Mill, *The Subjection of Women*.

A Man's World

Change has come about, and a good deal of ground has been conceded, if only inch by inch and with a long hard struggle. The records show that the ground has not been conceded gracefully. The records also show that the male, however gallantly he may have turned his phrases, if only because flattery was considered a suitable weapon against the female of the species, had no doubt that this was war. More often he became vituperative in fighting for his own rights. Like all people who are privileged by birth and long tradition, the idea of sharing could only mean giving up.

Today he has given up a good deal, and he likes to think he gave in gracefully, not to pressure, but to common sense and decency. It is a popular fallacy that only a few diehard bigots were ever really opposed to such obvious reforms as the granting of female suffrage, when in fact the idea was generally viewed with as much outrage and derision as the proposition that the earth was not flat, but round. And the fact that so many women should have been opposed to female suffrage shows how readily the average person accepts the position assigned by society. A slave becomes servile, the negro is ashamed of his black skin, the ostracized Jew clutches his moneybags for security.

Things change far more slowly than people suppose. Social reform does not necessarily mean a change of attitude, and the last citadel that a man will ever concede is the idea of his own superiority. Human beings have always been particularly slow to accept ideas that diminished their own absolute supremacy and importance (as, for instance, that the earth is not the centre of the universe). The fact that emotional attitudes, and ideas that have to do with the very nature of our own conception of ourselves are the slowest to change, means that social reform alone will have little immediate effect.

Anyone who imagines that the attitudes of today bear no relation to those of a few years ago has only to compare a few dicta. For instance, one of the favourite gibes of the opponents of the women's rights movement in the nineteenth century was that any woman who was interested in such questions must be lacking in feminine charms, in other words that she was making a fuss because she was unable to get what she really wanted in life—a man. Thus *Punch*[1] published the following verse in 1870:

> *The rights of Women who demand,*
> *Those women are but few:*
> *The greater part had rather stand*
> *Exactly as they do.*
>
> *Beauty has claims for which she fights*
> *At ease with winning arms;*
> *The women who want women's rights*
> *Want mostly, Women's charms.*

In her autobiography Simone de Beauvoir records that when she published *The Second Sex*, among the vituperation heaped upon her head by the press and private individuals were many suggestions that what was really 'wrong' with her was that she had never been properly fucked. Anthony Storr, in a book entitled *On Aggression* which appeared in 1968, has much to say about the females who insist upon taking up the rights they have won. 'The emancipation of women is an inescapable fact which will not be altered by artificial attempts to put the clock back,' he sighs, but states that 'solitary women exhibit a pseudo-masculine efficiency, a determined practical competence which they might expect or demand from a husband if only they had one'.

One of the most enduring ideas which men have passed down through the centuries in order to bolster their own feeling of superiority is the notion that women are intellectually inferior. It is an assumption that many influential thinkers have made quite baldly, without any inkling that there might be some need to prove such an assertion. One might almost say that men who have set the greatest store by their own intellect have tended to be misogynists in the same degree, as though they could only raise themselves up by pushing someone else down, until one reaches the final absurdity in Otto Weininger,[2] a young Austrian philosopher, who wrote a book at the end of the last century to prove that women were

---

[1] Quoted by Constance Rover in *The Punch Book of Women's Rights.*
[2] Otto Weininger, *Sex and Character.*

incapable of genius and virtually had no mind at all, and then committed suicide at the age of twenty-three because his own genius had not been sufficiently acclaimed on the book's publication. Leaving aside irascible male geniuses like Milton and Strindberg, the intellectual superiority of men has been assumed by churchmen and philosophers and the whole rabble of journalists and educationalists, politicians and mere husbands who follow happily in the rear. Anthony Storr is no exception, and claims that 'the undoubted superiority of the male sex in intellectual and creative achievement is related to their greater endowment of aggression . . . even when women have been given the opportunity to cultivate the arts and sciences, remarkably few have produced original works of outstanding quality, there have been no women of genius comparable to Michelangelo, Beethoven or Goethe'.[1]

Apart from the fact that there are remarkably few Beethovens and Michelangelos anyway, which is what makes them worthy of mention, it would seem to me that the ratio of opportunity to achievement is at least comparable, if not slightly in favour of the mindless ones. One wonders what the ratio was between men and women in the physics class at the Sorbonne when Marie Curie studied in Paris. However, Mr. Storr ignores such factors. But then, as Mary Wollstonecraft argued in defending the female intellect: 'The power of generalising ideas, of drawing comprehensive conclusions from individual observations . . . is not very common amongst men *or* women.'[2] (My italics.)

It is also an over-simplification to speak merely of opportunity for achievement. One has to consider motivation. Most people have latent abilities which they never use: this is partly inevitable since choosing to develop and exploit certain abilities must mean that others are neglected or lie dormant. The boy who is good at engineering and also has ability as a painter ultimately has to make a choice between two skills, and the choice will be determined as much by social factors and external pressures as by personal preference. Similarly, what women in general do now and have done in the past is not only the result of what they were allowed to do,

[1] Anthony Storr, *On Aggression*, p. 62.
[2] Mary Wollstonecraft, *A Vindication of the Rights of Woman*.

in the sense of there being no educational or employment prohibition, but of what was expected of them. Educationalists would surely agree that to allow a child to learn is only the half-way mark in almost all cases, most children have to be actively encouraged. A lazy boy will be prodded into ambition and aggression, but a girl has to be quite exceptional, to have that natural hunger for knowledge, that burning passion which may lead to great achievement, because no external motivation is provided. The ambition and aggression have to be generated totally from within, and have to be doubly powerful to break through two barriers, social prohibition and an opposite social expectation. Going back to the experiment with schoolchildren mentioned in my introduction, one could say that so far all girls have been treated as backward, and because this was the expectation, backward they have become.

In the patriarchal society that, for us, goes back as far as recorded history, female aggression has always been frowned on by males, since it means either insubordination or competition. In the words of Boccaccio:

> It is a hard and hateful thing to see proud men, not to speak of enduring them. But it is annoying and impossible to suffer proud women, because in general Nature has given men proud and high spirits, while it has made women humble in character and submissive, more apt for delicate things than for ruling. Therefore, it should not be surprising if God's wrath is swifter and the sentence more severe against proud women whenever it happens that they surpass the boundaries of their weakness.[1]

The wrath of a male god had long been invoked against disobedient women; the ancient Hebrews promised divine punishment for the disobedient woman who went against Nature, although it is difficult to see how women could rebel against a state of affairs which really was 'natural'. The idea that a woman who does not find total fulfilment in submitting herself utterly to the will of a husband and the demands of childbearing is somehow going against the natural order of things, is still with us. One may see the natural order as

[1] Boccaccio, *Concerning Famous Women*, Niobe (in the translation published by Allen and Unwin).

imposed from without, as Boccaccio here does, or conceive of it
as imposed from within, as the modern ethologists do, and as Freud
did when he spoke of women refusing to accept their own femininity, but in male eyes the offence is the same, as is the punishment—
masculine disapproval and a withdrawal of male love. One is
struck, regardless of intervening centuries, by the similarity of the
arguments, which, in spite of great developments in logic and the
sciences, remain illogical and circular, and by the similarity of tone,
which is usually aggrieved. Such words as 'annoying' and 'in-
sufferable' occurred frequently in the writings of people opposed
to an extension of women's rights in the nineteenth century, as they
do in the work of more purely emotional misogynists, such as
Strindberg. The same tone is recognizable in Mr. Storr, who
speaks of 'that insecure assertiveness which men find tiresome
when they have to work for female executives'. I think on the whole
I prefer the crude ridicule of *Punch*, or Pope, or Molière. Ridicule
has long been a favourite weapon, it can be cruel, often hits home,
but at least it is straightforward and unequivocal, the blows come
from the front and not from the back, and the man who deals them
is not all the time making out that he is not fighting.

Man has always known, if only subconsciously, that there was
a fight going on, and he blames woman for it on the grounds that
there would be no war if only she would give in. He is like a man
in a tussle who cannot get up because otherwise his vanquished
opponent would also get up, and might take another swing at him.
Victory is uneasy and demands eternal vigilance unless you can
come to terms and make peace with your enemy. And because man
has refused to abandon an inch of ground more than necessary,
having so much to lose, he has been afraid of the dormant power
he has subdued, and recognized woman as profoundly dangerous.
The idea of submission is inherent in the way we make love, man
on top, woman underneath, and I suppose most people brought
up in the Western cultural tradition would consider this the
'normal' way of making love. Malinowski's islanders called it the
'missionary' position and thought it highly unsatisfactory since it
afforded so little pleasure to the girls involved, though perhaps
more to the missionaries. It is significant that the Christian teaching

26

of the missionaries was also received without enthusiasm and with little comprehension: in a matrilineal society where paternity was not recognized or understood the inheritance of divinity through the male line meant nothing, nor of course did the immaculate conception.[1]

But for us the sexual act is inextricably bound up with the idea of submission, and when conditions are right any woman will at some time enjoy the element of submission, a voluptuous and willing abandon. But conditions are not always right. A submission that could have been voluntary is so no longer when one knows that it is enforced anyway. Man's trouble has always been to make the submission appear total enough, particularly in the bedchamber, because he demanded a slavish obedience devoid of sensuality. According to the ancient Hebrews God made three attempts to find a suitable mate for Adam, and even the third, the Eve who is familiar to all of us, was not without disastrous consequences. But the first wife, Lilith, was such as no man could be expected to cope with, and combined all the worst faults of medieval witches, George Sand and Mrs. Pankhurst:

> Adam and Lilith never found peace together; for when he wished to lie with her, she took offence at the recumbent posture he demanded. 'Why must I lie beneath you?' she asked. 'I also was made from dust, and am therefore your equal.' Because Adam tried to compel her obedience by force, Lilith, in a rage, uttered the magic name of God, rose into the air and left him.

This female virago then hovered on the outskirts of civilization, in those days not many miles away, and gave birth to demons, thus populating the world with evil. The abashed Adam appealed to God, who set about fashioning him a more suitable mate. But according to *Genesis Rabba*,[2] a midrash of the fifth century, God mistakenly allowed Adam to watch him construct the body of his second wife (the First Eve) and the sight caused Adam such disgust that God took her away and created the Second Eve. Nobody knows what became of the first.[3]

[1] Malinowski, *The Sexual Life of Savages.*
[2] From *Numeri Rabba*, a midrash on *Numbers* compiled in the twelfth century. Quoted by Robert Graves & Raphael Pata in *Hebrew Myths—The Book of Genesis*, p. 65.   [3] Ibid., p. 66.

Lilith is a recurring image of womanhood in a patriarchal society. She is mirrored in a passage of 'The Taboo of Virginity' by a later Jewish patriarch:

> Now upon this penis-envy follows that hostile embitterment displayed by women against men, never entirely absent in the relations between the sexes, the clearest indications of which are to be found in the writings and ambitions of 'emancipated' women. Ferenczi, in a palaeo-biological speculation, traces this enmity in women back to the era when differentiation between the sexes took place. . . . First of all, he believes, copulation was effected between two single organisms of the same kind, one of which, however, developed until it was the stronger and then forced the weaker to submit to sexual union; and the embitterment on account of this subjection is still an active predisposition in women today.[1]

Freud continually refers to the 'archaic' forces in women, but unlike Adam he is too civilized to attempt rape. Instead he transfers the male-female battle to within the woman herself. The male and female aspects of your character are in conflict, he tells woman, and it is up to you to see that the female aspect wins. Otherwise you are not a true woman and we cannot love you.

That Freud was defending an entrenched position just as much as the Hebrew patriarchs becomes obvious when we consider his objections to the ideas of John Stuart Mill, expressed in a letter to his fiancée, Martha Bernays:

> It is really a stillborn thought to send women into the struggle for existence exactly as men. If, for instance, I imagined my sweet gentle girl as a competitor it would only end in my telling her, as I did seventeen months ago, that I am fond of her and that I implore her to withdraw from the strife into the calm uncompetitive activity of my home. It is possible that changes in upbringing may suppress all a woman's tender attributes, needful of protection and yet so victorious, and that she can then earn a livelihood like men. It is also possible that in such an event one would not be justified in mourning the passing away of the most delightful thing the world can offer us—our ideal of womanhood. I believe that all reforming action in law and education would break down in front of the fact that, long before the age at which a man can earn a position in society, Nature has determined a woman's destiny through beauty, charm and sweet-

[1] Sigmund Freud, *Collected Papers*, Vol. 4, p. 231.

ness. Law and custom may have much to give women that has been
withheld from them, but the position of women will surely be what
it is: in youth an adored darling and in mature years a loved wife.[1]

Such banalities—and these sentiments were commonplace at the
time—are further confirmation of the sad conclusion that original
minds can be anything but original when it comes to accepting a
status quo which suits them and which helps to bolster their own
high opinion of themselves as persons. We shall see later that this
willingness to accept the contemporary roles of male and female
as right and inevitable led Freud into professional quagmires and
illogicalities which could easily have been avoided. He appears to
have been sincerely unaware of his personal bias, and being a man
of good will who had advocated that a woman should want to do
what man wanted her to do, follow the mirage for her own good,
he naturally found woman herself a perpetual enigma.

It was a common ploy to disarm woman with flattery, and get
her safely out of harm's way by placing her on a pedestal. Glad-
stone, in a letter on female suffrage written in 1892, said: 'The fear
I have is, lest we should invite her (woman) unwittingly to trespass
upon the delicacy, the purity, the refinement, the elevation of her
own nature, which are the present sources of its power.'[2] But much
more common was the tone of grievance, the assumption that by
trying to share male rights she somehow wanted to take them over
altogether. Although in reality this attitude stems from a far deeper
insecurity, and from the assumption that what one has always had
must somehow belong to one by right, it was usually justified on
the grounds that woman already had rights of her own. The idea
of usurpation crops up again and again. We find it in Rousseau:

'Others, not content to secure their rights, lead them to usurp ours;
for to make woman our superior in all the qualities proper to her
sex, and to make her our equal in all the rest, what is this but to
transfer to the woman the superiority which nature has given to her
husband?'[3]

---

[1] As quoted by Ernest Jones in *The Life and Work of Sigmund Freud*, p. 117. See
also *Letters of Sigmund Freud*.
[2] Quoted by Constance Rover, *Women's Suffrage and Party Politics in Britain 1866–
1914*, p. 120.
[3] *Emile* (in the translation published by Dent, Everyman Library).

Closer examination always reveals that female rights amount to the right to have children and the right to get what she wants by making herself particularly amiable to her husband, which is of course a very convenient arrangement as far as husbands are concerned. Without God to fashion a new mate out of thin air, the promise of material rewards makes a good substitute for the old Adam. If Lilith wants to be difficult about that recumbent posture she can always fly off in a rage and starve to death.

We admit that the most egalitarian lawmaker on earth cannot make it possible for a man to give birth to children, and we understand that it is desirable that men should have alternative fields of action, that they should feel powerful and important in their own right. But the unattainable and perhaps unenviable delights of the labour ward (if we are frank) are used as a cast-iron excuse for social inequality. 'If I cannot have a baby you cannot vote.' Thus Mr. Arnold Ward, opposing a female suffrage bill in the House of Commons in 1910:

> Innumerable unseen women will guard the entrance to those Division Lobbies tonight, and will be voting through us. It is now proposed, in addition, that they should have votes for themselves, thus practically having two votes, while we have none at all.[1]

Such tortuous logic is by no means dead. Sir John Newsom, defending his official report on education, which had been criticized for its retrograde attitude to the education of girls, wrote in 1964:

> The influence of women on events is exerted primarily in their role as wives and mothers, to say nothing of aunts and grandmothers. Even in employment outside the home, with the exception of schools and hospitals, this influence usually works by sustaining or inspiring the male. The most superficial knowledge of the way in which the affairs of Government, industry and commerce are conducted makes this quite plain. What infuriates a rather esoteric group of women is that they want to exert power both through men and also in their own right, and that this is almost impossible.[2]

These are the words of an authority on education today, of

[1] Constance Rover, *Women's Suffrage* etc., p. 40.
[2] Sir John Newsom in *The Observer* on 11th October 1964. Also quoted by Constance Rover, but personally recalled since I published a letter in the paper criticizing his views on girls' education.

a man who is helping to guide the paths of future men and women.

And it is with the question of education that the whole absurd question comes full circle. The justification for the sharp differentiation of male and female roles lies, in male eyes, in the natural order of things. When, therefore, either Rousseau or Newsom, both of whom have written at great length on the subject of education, advocate a different system of education for men and women one must ask oneself why any such course should be necessary, since natural aptitude would make women follow one line of action and men another. In the case of Rousseau the mask slips rather obviously. He may have been the great advocate of the natural man, but he was perfectly well aware that the whole industrial revolution was on the side of man, and that woman 'is dependent on our feelings, on the price we put upon her virtue, and the opinion we have of her charms and her deserts' even if he does add: 'Nature herself has decreed that woman, both for herself and her children, should be at the mercy of man's judgement.' It is for these reasons, in a sense for woman's own good, since the yoke is less painful if one does not fight it, that

> A woman's education must therefore be planned in relation to man. To be pleasing in his sight, to win his respect and love, to train him in childhood, to tend him in manhood, to counsel and console, to make his life pleasant and happy, these are the duties of woman for all time, and this is what she should be taught while she is young.[1]

No one would make quite such bald statements today, perhaps, but when one gets down to actual details remarkable similarities persist. In 1762 Rousseau wrote:

> Little girls always dislike learning to read and write, but they are always ready to learn to sew. They think they are grown up, and in imagination they are using their knowledge for their own adornment.[2]

In 1963, in a report rather aptly entitled *Half Our Future*,[3]

> We have not overlooked the fact that probably one of the easiest

[1] *Emile.*   [2] Ibid.
[3] *Half Our Future: a report of the Central Advisory Council for Education (England)*, H.M.S.O., 1963, p. 136. Sir John Newsom was chairman of the advisory council.

approaches, even with the most difficult girls, to more critical work in both housecraft and needlework lies in their natural interest in dress and personal appearance and social behaviour.

That girls should devote a considerable part of the curriculum to these crafts is justified by the fact that 'whether they marry early or not, they are likely to find themselves eventually making and running a home', just as Rousseau justified female education on the grounds that this would be her inevitable destiny. In so far as Rousseau thought that women should be educated at all beyond the craft of housekeeping, he and many others who followed after saw women as arbiters of 'good taste', and this idea has not died. In an industrial society where men are the breadwinners women are the consumers. In an age when specialized education has become an urgent necessity that is constantly talked about, it is curious to read Sir John Newsom advocating embroidery for half our future adults:

> Although we live in an era of high standard mass production of clothes, many women continue to find pleasure in needlework, including embroidery, as a recreational as well as a useful art . . . and as young married women they will soon be responsible for buying clothes for the family and furnishings for the home: they will need some foundation of taste, and an eye for finished workmanship and quality in materials, fashion and design.[1]

Turned round, both Rousseau's and Newsom's standpoint would appear to be that though boys do not show a natural aptitude for architectural engineering they love making mud pies. Or as dear, bumbling old Mr. Brooke told Casaubon in *Middlemarch*, 'Well, but now Casaubon, such deep studies, classics, mathematics, that kind of thing, are too taxing for a woman . . . there is a lightness about the feminine mind—a touch and go—music, the fine arts, that kind of thing—they should study those up to a certain point, women should; but in a light way you know.'

And although Newsom is of course ready to concede that the odd girl could devote more time to mathematics or physics, his emphasis on homemaking implies that a woman's education is still a way of making her a man's satellite:

[1] Ibid., p. 135.

One line of advance lies in courses built round broad themes of home making, to include not only material and practical provision but the whole field of personal relations in courtship, in marriage, and within the family—boy and girl friend, husband and wife, parents and children, young and old. At the age of thirteen and fourteen few girls are ready to explore these aspects of adult life and there are some aspects for which they will not be ready till after they have left school; but older girls can be brought to see that there is more to marriage than feeding the family and bathing the baby, and that they will themselves have a key role in establishing the standards of the home and in educating their children.[1]

To view this kind of indoctrination as a study specifically designed for girls seems to me to be not very different from Rousseau's statement that a woman's studies 'should be thoroughly practical ... beyond the range of her immediate duties, should be directed to the study of men, or the acquirement of that agreeable learning whose sole end is the formation of taste ... she must have a thorough knowledge of man's mind; not an abstract knowledge of the mind of man in general, but the mind of those men who are about her, either by law or custom.' Or is that last sentence of Newsom's so different from Rousseau's: 'In talking to a young girl you need not make her afraid of her duties. ... Show them that these same duties are the source of their pleasures and the basis of their rights.'[2] We already know what those rights are and were—to rule the world by rocking the cradle and inspiring her male.

I hope I have said enough in this introductory chapter to justify the analysis that follows. I am not speaking about conditions that are past and done with, but about a tradition which perpetuates itself in different guises. Only a few months ago, in 1969, Dr. Edmund Leach told a conference at Keele that it was time we stopped educating our women like men and producing 'imitation second class males', because it was getting too difficult to get anyone willing to do domestic chores (*The Times*, 26th July 1969). It has been objected that anything which perpetuates itself for so long must have a basis of truth, that if both Freud and the ancient Hebrews formulated the same idea there must be something

[1] Ibid., p. 137.   [2] *Emile.*

in it. Not necessarily, and it may be that we should first examine
Freud and the ancient Hebrews before going on to the object
of their remarks. This is what I suggest we should do, if only
to clear the jungled path a little. John Stuart Mill met this
objection a hundred years ago and I would like to quote it here:

> . . . people flatter themselves that the rule of mere force is ended; that
> the law of the strongest cannot be the reason of existence of anything
> which has remained in full operation down to the present time.
> However any of our present institutions may have begun, it can
> only, they think, have been preserved to this period of advanced
> civilization by a well-grounded feeling of its adaption to human
> nature, and conduciveness to the general good. They do not under-
> stand the great vitality and durability of institutions which place
> right on the side of might; how intensely they are clung to; how the
> good as well as the bad propensities and sentiments of those who
> have power in their hands, become identified with retaining it. . . .[1]

On the whole we have less faith in enlightened progress than
Mill's generation. Perhaps just because our faith in civilization has
been badly shaken we cling all the more desperately to what we
hope is our fundamental human nature, our basic and even traditional identities as man or woman, and our only guides are the
roles that man and woman have traditionally played. When things
go wrong we feel lost and tend to think that it is because we have
departed too far from tradition, and try that much harder to
conform to the image. Which is only a mirage.

[1] John Stuart Mill, *The Subjection of Women.*

34

II

A Man's God

Although we are accustomed to think of God as masculine our world did not begin in the Garden of Eden. Earlier creation myths give an importance to the figure of woman which in *Genesis* is accorded to man (although even the Old Testament still shows signs of an earlier matriarchy). When one talks of the matriarchy of prehistory one can mean little more than this: woman, particularly as childbearer, was important, and descent was naturally matrilineal because that was the way it was first understood. We still find matrilocal marriage in the Old Testament, in Samson's marriage to Delilah, for example.

Adam was made God's overseer after the Creation, but earlier gardens of delight were ruled over by females: the Greek goddess Hera inhabited the Garden of the Hesperides, guarded by the serpent Ladon; Gilgamesh went to a Sumerian paradise ruled over by Siduri, Goddess of Wisdom. Significantly, Hera's garden was destroyed by Heracles with the connivance of Zeus, whilst in later versions of the Gilgamesh epic Siduri had been ousted by the Sun-god Shamash, whom she had appointed guardian of the garden, and degraded to the position of a mere barmaid at a neighbouring tavern. We see here the male wish to usurp the power of an overbearing female figure, by combined strength or cunning. Malinowski,[1] whose Trobriand Islanders represented a similarly early stage of development, with creation associated exclusively with woman, quotes the myth of a sort of female Prometheus: woman had created the sun, but kept back a little of the fire in order to cook, hiding the fire in her vagina when she was not

[1] Malinowski: *The Sexual Life of Savages.*

35

using it. But man discovered her hiding place and stole it. Perhaps it would be more appropriate to regard this story as the origin of the male figure of Prometheus, with man stealing power, not from any gods, but from woman. It could also represent the extension of human activity beyond mere domestic cooking, with this whole new sphere being male, whilst woman remains at the hearth!

Originally, and it was inevitable that this should have been so, the world began with a woman, though early serpent gods also figure largely. According to Greek myth the goddess Eurynome was impregnated by the wind in the shape of a serpent and laid the World Egg.[1] The serpent probably had phallic associations, but these are indirect, man does not really figure in the Creation. The serpent who beguiled Eve was in fact an earlier god. Perhaps he owed his divinity to the fact that he appeared to create and re-create himself, by sloughing his skin. Certainly snakes are both insidious and dangerous. Menstruation, according to one primitive belief, begins when a woman is bitten by a snake.

Birth and death are the elementary facts of life, but because of the way we live now they are pushed into the background and we are hardly aware of them except as the almost abstract limits of personal existence. Pregnancy is carefully concealed, the dead body is discreetly removed by an undertaker. People hardly ever die or give birth in public, for death and parturition people are removed to hospitals and nursing homes where only the closest relatives will dare or be allowed to penetrate. The rest of us stay away until it is all over, when we may take the trouble to write congratulations or condolences, a ritual which is so detached, so obviously mere formality, that even this hardly seems worth doing. Why disturb the even tenor of 'normality' at all? The new mother will be happily preoccupied, the newly bereaved will want to forget as fast as possible, so why provide a painful reminder?

But the more simple the community, the more birth and death become public events in which all share. And the more limited the horizons, and the possible range of individual experience, the

[1] For early creation myths mentioned in this chapter see Robert Graves and Raphael Pata, *Hebrew Myths—the Book of Genesis.*

greater the importance attributed to arrival and departure, birth
and death. And to the savage mind nothing, surely, can be more
important or more magical than the arrival of a new human being,
the creation of someone like oneself, it is a positive manifestation
that outbalances the mysterious terror of death.

Since woman is usually weaker than man in physical strength one
must assume that the importance once accorded to her was due to
her role as childbearer, and that man considered her creative role
as all-important in this respect because he was unaware of his own
part in the reproductive process. It is only when man has understood that by laying a woman he impregnates her, and that he is
the physical father of the child she bears, that he can begin to think
of himself as creator, relegate woman to the role of a mere vessel,
and acquire either the motivation or the assurance for domination.
In the Trobriand Islanders Malinowski did in fact discover a
society where people were unaware of any connection between the
sex act and paternity, and although Malinowski himself denied that
one could assume that this was a phase in all human development,
it is really more logical to assume it than not. Most relations
between cause and effect have had to be discovered at some stage
if they are not immediately obvious, and in a society where all
women have sexual intercourse from puberty, all marry early and
bear children, cause and effect are by no means that clear, any more
than one would expect a simple savage to deduce that the world
is round from the fact that the sun rises in the east each morning
and sets in the west. He has his own explanation for the phenomenon. Thus Malinowski found that the exception could easily
prove the rule, any rule. His attempts to explain the facts of life
were met with derision. How could what he said be true, they
asked, since the woman in the next hut had been married for many
years and had never borne a child? On the other hand there was
a single woman, so ugly that no man would ever condescend to
lie with her, who had had four children. . . .

The assumption tends to be confirmed by a comparison between early myths of creation and the beliefs of the Trobriand
Islanders. For instance, the islanders thought that the spirits of the
dead, after spending some time on another island, returned as

37

spirit babies on driftwood and entered a woman when she was bathing. The Greeks, also islanders, saw a connection between procreation and sea water: the goddess Eurynome danced upon the waves, and stirred up the wind which impregnated her. The Trobrianders also believed that a woman had to be impregnated in order to conceive and bear a child, not so that her seed should be fertilized by a man, but in order that the vaginal opening should be large enough. Thus, although a virgin had to be deflowered in order to bear a child, it did not have to be by a man. In their mythology a primeval woman is always imagined to bear children without the intervention of a male partner, but not without the vagina being opened in some way. The mother of the legendary hero Tudava lived quite alone in a grotto by the seashore, and was sleeping under a stalactite when the drops of water pierced her vagina.

A society such as this must obviously be matrilineal, but that is a long way from being a matriarchy in the sense of actual female dominance, which would depend on a variety of factors which are not necessarily also present, or not in the right combination. Certainly the Trobrianders do not present us with a picture of awful bossy females and timid insecure males. No society is ideal, and the combination of matriliny with patrilocy appears to have given rise to a certain amount of conflict, since a father's affection was for the children he had nursed, even though he did not recognize those children as his own, whilst his duty was to his sister's children, who were relative strangers but who could make certain claims on him, and over whom he had a certain amount of authority. What was lacking in this society was male domination, both over women and children, and perhaps this is all that the much vaunted matriarchy ever was, or could be. It not only made for a minimum of sexual repression and conflict, but also, since there was no authoritarian father figure, for a minimum of conflict between the generations.

The motivation for male domination over the female is intimately connected with the idea of paternity. Once a man knows that there is a physical link between himself and the child in his woman's womb, that, provided no other man has been allowed to impregnate his woman, the child will definitely be his, a continuation of himself, all kinds of things become possible. The idea of personal continuity is born, if man can only control his woman he becomes, in a sense, immortal. Power and property can be passed down through his sons and so clutched beyond the grave. By playing down the all-important role that woman plays in procreation, by regarding her as a mere vessel in which he plants his seed, man discovers and exploits a new sense of power, a new domination over his environment. He can pass both his name and his acquired wealth down to his sons, who in their turn will pass it down to their sons, and thus cheat death. It makes it worthwhile to become hardworking and acquisitive instead of vacillating between fear of the unknown and a relaxed enjoyment of temporary pleasures, to become an aggressive conqueror, to stake a claim on land and hold on to it at all costs. The male seed is of tremendous importance in the Old Testament, lines of male descent are recorded in great detail, generation by generation, and the woman is no more than a bearer of male children. If a woman proves barren the Old Testament male will soon turn to a concubine or take a second wife, usually with the connivance or humble acceptance of his barren woman, who recognizes her own inadequacy.

But all this motivation for living in a certain way depends on one thing, making sure that the child in the womb is really yours, and that you are the father. And since no man can control all other men it is primarily the woman he must control, mentally or physically. Mental control means taboos, and the advantage of taboos is that up to a certain point they control other men as well. Physical control means harems, purdah, chastity belts, the punishment of adultery by death and, I suppose one could add, the kind of economic sanctions which have so long flourished in our own society, where the woman taken in adultery would not be stoned but merely turned out of house and home to starve, with no form of legal redress.

In a book entitled *Purity and Danger* Mary Douglas argues that there are less sexual taboos in a society where the male can enforce his domination directly, and where society allows a man to punish his wife with direct physical force. She quotes the Walbiri of

A Man's God

Central Australia as an example of direct physical control:

> A married woman usually lives at a distance from her father and brothers. This means that though she has a theoretical claim to their protection, in practice it is null. She is in the control of her husband. As a general rule if the female sex were completely subject to the male, no problem would be posed by the principle of male dominance. It could be enforced ruthlessly and directly wherever it applied. This seems to be what happens among the Walbiri. For the least complaint or neglect of duty Walbiri women are beaten or speared. No blood compensation can be claimed for a wife killed by her husband, and no one has the right to intervene between husband and wife. . . . However energetically they may try to seduce one another's wives the men are in perfect accord on one point. They are agreed that they should never allow their sexual desires to give an individual woman bargaining power or scope for intrigue.
>
> These people have no beliefs concerning sex pollution. Even menstrual blood is not avoided, and there are no beliefs that contact with it brings danger . . . when a man poaches on another's sexual preserves he knows what he risks, a fight and possible death. The system is perfectly simple. There are conflicts between men, but not between principles.[1]

If one looks at our own civilization one can see a gradual shift from direct physical control to a system of complex and subtle taboos. The shift from external to internal controls that one sees between old Jewish and later Christian morality, the Old Testament and the New. Killing a woman taken in adultery represents direct physical control, but Christ's prohibition against committing adultery in your heart is a form of taboo, and to be significantly effective taboos must involve the minds of men as well as women. In the Middle Ages it was still acceptable to beat one's wife or daughter, but by the nineteenth century there was an effective network of moral taboos which controlled the wives and daughters of the upper and middle class (enforced, of course, by the underlying realities of economic dependence and social ostracism for those that strayed). So those same upper and middle classes shrank in horror at the idea of physical punishment for women. Sons might get beaten, but girls and ladies were always treated with kid gloves. Gallantry and polite deference were the order of the day. Only

[1] Mary Douglas, *Purity and Danger*, pp. 141-2.

amongst the working classes, where there was no social ostracism to fear, and where married women were not economically dependent in the same way, since they had to work anyhow, did men still resort to beating their wives, and were duly admonished by their social betters. In the Victorian novel the washerwoman with the black eye administered by her drunken husband was visible proof for the ladies with leisure to read, of the barbarity, the lack of refined feeling, in the working classes.

The voice of God is the voice of man. Religion does not only embody human belief, it embodies the attitudes, the moral and social codes of the human beings who celebrate that religion, of the priests and scribes who give it body and reality. The voice of the lawmaker is more likely to inspire unquestioning obedience if it can thunder out from behind a terrifying mask, or reveal its wishes from above. The male Jehovah is a stern Hebrew patriarch who leaves us in no doubt about the position of woman. Far from being the mother of all the races of men, the natural order has been reversed, and woman is born out of man, no more than a single male rib. One account of the Creation in a Judean version of *Genesis* is particularly contemptuous: 'He made a garden in Eden, also a man named Adam to be its overseer, and planted it with trees. He then created all beasts, birds, creeping things; and lastly woman.'[1] Since woman's only function was procreation, the greatest curse possible was for her to be barren, and the greatest favour that Jehovah could bestow on her was to make her unexpectedly fruitful in her old age, as he did Sarah and Rachel. But always his reason for bestowing such a favour was in order to create special sons, like Isaac, and Benjamin and Joseph, as later he was to bestow his most special favour on a woman not too old but too young and pure to conceive in order to create his most special Son of all. Had Mary not been a Virgin the lineage of the Son of God would have been in doubt.

However, just in case woman should get ideas above her station by the high honour of giving birth to such great males (and humble Mary calls herself a handmaiden) the full responsibility for the Fall

[1] Robert Graves & Raphael Pata, *Hebrew Myths* etc., p. 21.

is heaped upon her shoulders. 'I will greatly multiply thy sorrow and thy conception; in sorrow thou shalt bring forth children; and thy desire shall be to thy husband, and he shall rule over thee.'

Just as Pandora let loose old age and vice, the evils of the world, so Eve was made responsible for man's mortality and fall from grace. This interpretation of the origin of undesirable things was to prove very useful for a long time to come, and it served a double purpose. On the one hand it allowed man to assert his domination that much more forcibly, he literally had the whip hand and could go on punishing woman for what she was supposed to have done, thus justifying his domination, and on the other hand it allowed him to externalize all flaws and weaknesses in himself and make woman the embodiment of them, leaving himself strong and intact and morally superior. And since sexuality is always the Achilles heel in this arrangement not only do the strongest taboos surround sex, but it is woman's sexuality that he most loathes and fears.

That the apocryphal Jehovah should have made two botched attempts at creating a mate for Adam before Eve,[1] suggests that the men who recorded this interpretation of prehistory had considerable difficulty in providing an archetypal woman who would fit the bill, almost as much as Jehovah. On the one hand they had to give Adam a suitable wife, submissive and weak, someone who would serve as an image for nice Jewish girls about to cross the threshold of matrimony so that they did not get above themselves. On the other hand the first woman had to be responsible for all the evils and disasters that had overtaken the world since the Creation. Could one image really tally with the other? Admittedly a weak nature would allow her to be beguiled by Satan, but if man was really better and stronger, how come that he had allowed himself to be led astray by a mere woman? Surely that made him the weaker of the two? It was a dilemma that was to face Milton later, and, stern Puritan that he was, he also knew that the fatal flaw was sex. The rabbis tried to get round the problem by embodying the demonic qualities in another, earlier wife, who had nothing to do with the submissive woman who became the mother of the human race. They took over the Babylonian-Assyrian demon Lilit

[1] Ibid., p. 66.

or Lilu, and made her the first wife of Adam, Lilith. The following passage comes from *Yalqut Reubeni*, a collection of kabbalistic comments on the *Pentateuch* compiled by R. Reuben ben Hoshke Cohen in Prague in the seventeenth century:

> God then formed Lilith, the first woman, just as he had formed Adam, except that He used filth and sediment instead of pure dust. From Adam's union with this demoness, and with another like her named Naamah, Tubal Cain's sister, sprang Asmodeus and innumerable demons that still plague mankind. Many generations later, Lilith and Naamah came to Solomon's judgement seat, disguised as harlots of Jerusalem.[1]

Harlot and demoness, they are one and the same thing. Or rather one should say, harlot, demoness and unnaturally rebellious woman are one and the same thing, for Lilith was really the first example of that awful creature later to be dubbed the 'emancipated' woman, or the woman who likes to imagine herself to be emancipated, like a man, which she is not, of course. 'Why must I lie beneath you?' asked Lilith in the twelfth-century midrash *Numeri Rabba*, when she refused the missionary position in the act of love. 'I also was made from dust, and am therefore your equal.' But by the seventeenth century the rabbinical scholars had found an answer to this awkward question: she was created from 'filth and sediment instead of pure dust' like Adam. However, the insubordinate creature flew off in a rage and even the intervention of God could not induce her to come back.[2] That the evils of the world should have gone on multiplying since is explained by the fact that Lilith 'escaped the curse of death which overtook Adam, since they had parted long before the Fall. Lilith and Naamah not only strangle infants but also seduce dreaming men, any one of whom, sleeping alone, may become their victim'.[3] According to the *Babylonian Talmud*, compiled in Babylonia in about A.D. 500 and written partly in Hebrew, partly in Aramaic.

Thus Lilith and Naamah, like the Greek Lamiae before them and the medieval Christian succubi which were to follow, controlled men's bodies even as they slept, such was their evil power. That they should strangle infants is significant. Witches were also held

[1] Ibid., p. 65.   [2] Ibid., p. 65.   [3] Ibid., p. 66.

responsible for the deaths of children in Christian Europe. Man splits the image of woman in two once more: the good woman is associated with motherhood and purity, the bad with uncontrollable sexuality and, since she is the opposite of the good mother, the death of infants. By creating two wives for Adam (if we leave out of account the middle wife, only briefly alluded to and too physically repulsive to Adam for further relations, since he had watched her being created) we see the dissociation of wickedness and sexuality from motherhood, which reached its peak in the image of the Virgin Mary. Eve was to be the mother of mankind, whilst Lilith merely gave birth to demons and wickedness. Obviously the ultimate in the image of the good mother was one who had never known or roused sexual lust. (Incidentally, the idea that Adam could only find a wife attractive when he had not watched her being made, i.e. when he had slept during her creation, an idea reiterated in several midrashes where the First, abandoned, Eve is mentioned, suggests that female charms exist only in the mind of man and are largely fantasmal, as the belief in demonic witchcraft and extreme puritanism constantly emphasize.)

The rabbinical scholars went on dotting the *i*'s and crossing their *t*'s. If the idea was to make woman responsible for all the evils of the world, how come that Adam had fathered both Abel and Cain, the first murderer? The theological answer was quite simply that he had not. The *Vitae Adae et Evae*, an apocryphal book of Jewish origin, probably first century B.C., which is extant in Greek, Latin and Slavonic versions, dealt with this new flaw in the patriarchal morality. According to this book Abel was fathered by Adam but Cain was the son of the Serpent Samael, who is of course Satan, making Eve something of a whore. But Eve, being Eve and not Lilith, was very contrite. 'Alas, Adam, I have sinned! Banish me from the light of your life. I will go westward, there to await death.' But the devoted Adam followed her into the wilderness, and four angels assisted at the difficult delivery.[1] For once it might have been preferable to stone the adultress to death, though it would have given rise to further theological difficulties, such as an adequate explanation for later evils.

[1] Ibid., p. 85.

Woman as a source of danger, as a repository of externalized evil, is an image that runs through patriarchal history. She is witch, demoness, scarlet woman, schemer, and her power in the minds of men usually increases in inverse proportion to her actual power in the world of reality. In time of unnatural or unprecedented disasters, *cherchez la femme*. The very fact that she could only exert her own will through man made her dangerous, because if she succeeded it meant that man had virtually no will at all. Those men who later opposed the movement for women's rights on the grounds that women could get what they wanted, and should be content to get what they wanted, through their menfolk must have been very sure of their power of resistance, because otherwise their worst fears would have come to pass, with women having all the power and men none at all.

A woman who is allowed to get what she wants may be a confounded nuisance, but she is far less dangerous than the woman who has to work by insidious means, by worming her way inside a man and exploiting his weakness. And yet this is precisely what man has told woman to do. And myth, religion and ancient superstitions reveal that man was well aware of the danger to which he was exposing himself, but did not know how to cope with it.

However enslaved and subdued, a woman can manipulate a man if she is the object of his desire, and she knows it. It is not open rebellion that constitutes the real danger, you can tame a shrew by giving her a sound beating before stopping her mouth with a kiss, preach sermons against female pride, disobedience and gossip, laugh at bluestockings and militant feminists. The real danger is the woman who is too cunning and subtle to do any such thing, who can exploit her attractions and sway a man so that he is not even aware of being used. And however much man may subject woman to his will, however loudly he screams 'harlot!' the fact remains that the weakness will inevitably recur, so he has to double and treble the sexual taboos, because his potential downfall always lies in his animal lusts. The Hebraic tradition moves from a strong assertion of the double standard to a position where all sex is devalued, to the Essenes and Christians who advocated celibacy as the ideal.

A Man's God

The fear is expressed as a fear of emasculation, of loss of strength. Thus the Hindus and ancient Chinese believed that a man should abstain from sexual intercourse in order to conserve his strength. The Victorians also believed that an expenditure of semen either through intercourse or masturbation had a debilitating effect and that too many ejaculations could lead to madness and physical collapse. Most tribes have a taboo on women before hunting expeditions or a battle, but the fear, when there are strong sexual taboos, goes far beyond a fear of a loss of mere physical strength. Total emasculation, implying an absolute loss of will is the fear, a reversal of the male-dominant situation. In the Old Testament we have the story of Samson and Delilah, which provides an awful warning of what can happen to the epitome of masculine strength when he allows himself to be taken in by the wiles of a woman. The same fate befell another hero of legendary strength. This is how Boccaccio tells the story:

Iole, the daughter of King Eurytus of Aetolia, was the most beautiful among the girls of that country. There are some who say that she was loved by Hercules, the master of the world. It is said that Eurytus promised him his daughter in marriage but later refused when his son dissuaded him. Angered by this, Hercules bitterly waged war against him and killed him. After conquering the country he took his beloved Iole to himself. She was certainly moved more by her father's death than by love of her husband. Desiring vengeance, with marvelous and constant slyness she covered her feelings towards him with false love. With caresses and a certain artful wantonness she made Hercules love her so much that she could see very well that he would not deny her anything she might ask. For this reason, before anything else she told that powerful man to put aside the club with which he had tamed the monsters and to remove the skin of the Nemean lion, which was a sign of his strength, as if she were afraid of her lover, who was so rough because of his clothes. She made him put aside the poplar wreath and his quiver and arrows. This not being sufficient for her heart she moved more daringly against her defenceless enemy with weapons prepared in advance. First she asked him to adorn the fingers of his hands with rings, anoint his head with Cyprian unguents, comb his shaggy hair, anoint his rough beard with nard, and adorn himself with girlish garlands and the Naeonian headdress. Then she made him dress in dainty purple clothes, believing that she, a young woman armed with her deceit, had performed a greater

46

deed by weakening with luxury a robust man, than if she had killed him with steel or poison. Certainly, thinking that she had not sufficiently satisfied her wrath, she brought that man, who had given himself up to luxury, to such a pass that he would sit like a woman among other common women and tell the story of his labors. Taking the distaff, he would spin wool, and his fingers, which had been hard enough to kill serpents when he was still a baby, now at a vigorous age, in fact his prime, were being softened by spinning wool.[1]

Hercules with a woman's distaff is the ultimate in humiliation. The moral of this story is: 'We must therefore be vigilant and arm our hearts with great strength, so that we are not overcome against our wishes.'

Milton's Samson feels himself justly punished for having allowed himself to be dominated by a woman. To become 'effeminate', to be ruled by that lowly thing, a woman, is far worse than to be honourably killed in battle, or even than enslavement to a hated enemy:

> *But foul effeminacy held me yok't*
> *Her Bond-slave; O indignity, O blot*
> *To Honour and Religion! servil mind*
> *Rewarded well with servil punishment!*
> *The base degree to which I now am fall'n,*
> *These rags, this grinding, is not yet so base*
> *As was my former servitude, ignoble,*
> *Unmanly, ignominious, infamous,*
> *True slavery, and that blindness worse than this,*
> *That saw not how degenerately I serv'd.*[2]

From the anthropological point of view the fates of Hercules and Samson are interesting because they seem to contain a warning against the dangers of exogamy. Both Delilah and Iole belonged to hostile tribes, and Hercules went so far as to take his bride by force, through the conquest of war. Other proud male warriors have been undone by sexual passion, Holofernes, for instance.

In the nineteenth century men also felt threatened by sexual attraction, the moral was also 'leave it alone, or at least be on your

---

[1] Boccaccio, *Concerning Famous Women* (Allen & Unwin).
[2] John Milton, *Samson Agonistes*.

guard'; but because they had replaced the attributes of male physical power and domination by wealth and property, by economic domination, the Delilah of nineteenth-century fiction was a courtesan who induced her lover to load her with houses and jewels and thus brought him to the verge of bankruptcy, another form of emasculation. In popular parlance the Victorian word for sexual climax was to 'spend', and it was important not to spend more than you could afford.

Contact with woman weakens and emasculates a man, has to be avoided before masculine pursuits like hunting and fighting, and must be properly regulated to avoid excess. Whereas male strength and power, including sexuality, is regarded as a fixed and easily exhaustible quantity, woman is thought to be all appetite, sexually insatiable, and will emasculate him by sucking him dry; she may even possess a *vagina dentata* and castrate him. If he avoids intercourse the powers of evil take over, she visits him in his sleep as a succubus and causes him to spill his seed in spite of himself. Margaret Mead gives an example of this attitude:

> Among the Arapesh the problem is seen not as maintenance of potency but as resistance of seduction by strong positively sexed women. 'She will hold your cheeks, you will hold her breasts, your skin will tremble, you will sleep together, she will steal part of your body fluid, later she will give it to the sorcerer and you will die. . . .' No Arapesh came to the door of the field clinic asking for medecine to restore his potency; instead he came for emetics to undo the harm that sorcery—following seduction—had done him.[1]

Significantly, Freud also regarded the female as sexually insatiable, though he did not express it quite so bluntly: woman, he said, is incapable of renouncing her instinctual demands in the interests of civilization. Some observers have regarded sexual taboos as a natural form of birth control, but much more important in the limitation of sexual activity is the way it reduces sexual conflict between males in a community. If pregnant or menstruating women are untouchable, if there is no lovemaking on certain days and before or after certain events, a man can leave his woman unguarded with an easy mind on those occasions. Desmond Morris would say that marriage harked back to the time when our ancestors

[1] Margaret Mead, *Male and Female.*

went off hunting in a pack like wolves, leaving their females behind; Freud also bases his theory of civilization on a fair sharing out of females. But taboos appear to be necessary to enforce the sexual pact and most men tend to see woman as the temptress who seduces him, or tries to seduce him into breaking his honourable male pact. *The Two Gentlemen of Verona*, for instance, is based on the idea of honour between men, and the young woman's feelings are simply not consulted at all—she might as well be a desirable horse being passed to and fro. Of course, if woman is too thoroughly excluded from 'civilization' or the power and rewards of community life, she tends to be a disruptive influence, she will have an interest in making men break the pacts they have made, in using cunning and intrigue, in playing off one man against another. Thus, as Freud said, woman *is* hostile to the demands of civilization—when the civilization is a totally masculine, the only one that Freud recognized. It is an ironic fact that man, having tried to confine woman more and more to the bedroom, should then complain that woman is always trying to drag him back to bed. What else is the poor soul supposed to do, to avoid dying of sheer boredom? Rousseau, for example, firmly believed that woman should exist solely for man's pleasure, and yet he complained loudly of the strongly sexed woman who would not wait for man to make the advances. If women were not restrained by modesty and shame from making sexual advances, he wrote, the 'human race would perish through the very means ordained for its continuance'.[1] Because in strange contradiction to all that he has said about her natural function as the submissive and subordinate mate of man, she seems to be nothing of the sort:

> Women so easily stir a man's senses and fan the ashes of a dying passion, that if philosophy ever succeeded in introducing this custom into any unlucky country, especially if it were a warm country where more women are born than men, the men, tyrannised over by the women, would at last become their victims, and would be dragged to their deaths without the least chance of escape.
> Female animals are without this sense of shame, but what of that? Are their desires as boundless as those of women, who are curbed by this shame?[2]

[1] *Emile.*   [2] Ibid.

49

So female modesty becomes a kind of bridle for the protection of men.

The fear of the uncontrolled woman keeps recurring in one form or another. Today the modern woman, armed with 'the Pill', is often regarded as rapacious because she is no longer deterred from unbridled sexuality by the fear of unwanted children. The simple fact that a woman may also have natural appetites, which if normally satisfied, then lie dormant for a while, is rarely understood. The Victorian attitude which insists that woman has no appetite at all and must make no demands is a defence against the fear of the opposite extreme—that woman is *all* appetite, *all* demands. The opposite of domination is to be dominated, and bands of Amazons, women who use men only for one act after having conquered them in war, and who slay all boys at birth, haunt the minds of men in mythology. It is a hidden fear that somehow, if they are only given a chance, women will suddenly do as they have been done by. Even the Trobriand Islanders had a myth of the insatiable woman, where women killed men with pleasure (but perhaps they secretly rather relished the thought!). They told Malinowski about an island inhabited by beautiful naked women who pounced on any stranded sailor and used him as a sexual instrument. Boy babies were sexually misused and died of exhaustion long before maturity, and although a few daring travellers claimed to have visited the island and lived to tell the tale, no white man had so far survived the ordeal and returned to confirm the existence of the island![1]

In a patriarchal society male dominance must be maintained at all costs, because the person who dominates cannot conceive of any alternative but to be dominated in turn. And the sex act becomes symbolic of that situation—the man who lies on top of the woman is literally in the 'superior' position, and by doing so he controls the whole of the sex act. He is active, decides the moment of climax, and passivity is more or less enforced on the woman. If denial of sexual pleasure to woman is part of his culture (as it was in nineteenth-century Europe) he is in the most advantageous position to ensure that she does not approach orgasm herself, being pinned

[1] Malinowski, *The Sexual Life of Savages.*

down and unable to move effectively. I am not of course saying that a nineteenth-century husband would deliberately deny his wife physical pleasure—merely that the traditional 'missionary position' does not make it easy for a woman to discover and exploit her own sexuality and would therefore perpetuate the current idea of universal female frigidity. Whilst in a more barbarous age the man would simply pounce on his woman and get it over with, without consulting her.

The sex act is an effective symbol because it is so basic and animal, and can be considered 'natural'—so if it is 'natural' for a man to lie on top of a woman it would therefore follow that male domination is also part of the natural order. Several Hebrew midrashes, including *Genesis Rabba* and a Palestinian midrash of the eighth or early ninth century, attribute the Flood as the result of God's anger when this natural order was upset:

> He then commanded Noah to sit beside the door of the ark and observe each creature as it came towards him. Such as crouched down in his presence were to gain admittance; such as remained standing must be excluded. Some authorities say that according to God's orders, if the male lorded it over the female of his own kind, both were admitted, but not otherwise. And that He gave these orders because it was no longer men alone that committed bestiality. The beasts themselves rejected their own mates: the stallion mounted the she-ass; the jack-ass, the mare; the dog, the she-wolf; the serpent, the tortoise; and so forth—moreover, females frequently lorded it over males. God had decided to destroy all creatures whatsoever, except those that obeyed His will.[1]

One sees that over and over again the angry male Jehovah is allowed to wipe the slate clean and start again if things do not work out the way he ordained. One cannot but be surprised at the capacity for 'natural' creatures to behave in a thoroughly 'unnatural' manner. It is rather like saying 'This is a free country and anyone who says otherwise will be liquidated'.

Religion is not only a way in which the male projects a vision of the world as he would wish it to be and expresses his attitudes with regard to himself in relation to others and the universe at large, a

[1] Robert Graves & Raphael Pata, *Hebrew Myths* etc., p. 112.

voice he uses in order to lay down a moral law. Religion is in itself a male cult, and like initiation ceremonies, is specifically designed to exclude women and give the male a compensatory activity for the female one of childbearing.

Importance can be given to a group activity if certain sectors of the community are excluded. Many groups derive their whole mystique from their exclusiveness, and as far as some forms of group activity are concerned one is bound to conclude that their *only* significance lies in the careful exclusion of non-members. One thinks of freemasonry, or the all-male clubs of London. Captain Cook found that Polynesian women (who also ate their meals apart, but were quite happy to eat with the European sailors as long as their menfolk did not discover their transgression) were not allowed to enter places of worship. Margaret Mead describes initiation rites, involving noise-making instruments such as bamboo flutes and hollow logs which the womenfolk were not allowed to see. A great mystique surrounded these rites, but the whole ritual could actually only work with the collusion of the women who were, so to speak, careful not to look. Thus, like faithful readers of the modern woman's magazine, they knew one of the recipes for a stable marriage, which is to bolster the male's sense of self-importance. Margaret Mead goes further, and sees all male activity, not just initiation rites, as a form of male compensation for the inability to bear children:

> In every known human society, the male's need for achievement can be recognized. Men may cook or weave or dress dolls or hunt humming-birds, but if such activities are appropriate occupations for men, then the whole society, men and women alike, vote them as important. When the same occupations are performed by women, they are regarded as less important. In a great number of human societies men's sureness of their sex roles is tied up with their right, or ability, to practise some activity that women are not allowed to practise. Their maleness, in fact, has to be underwritten by preventing women from entering some field or performing some feat. Here may be found the relationship between maleness and pride; that is, a need for prestige that will outstrip the prestige which is accorded to any woman.[1]

[1] Margaret Mead, *Male and Female*.

If one agrees with this estimate, one would at first glance appear to be recognizing the need for a traditional approach to the separate roles of men and women. It would seem to be a plea for woman to stand back in mature wisdom and relinquish any claims to share in male power and activity. But the point is surely, not only that our modern world has a far greater variety of tempting opportunities to offer than the limited life of a primitive community, but that the society in which we find ourselves today no longer attaches great prestige or importance to childbearing, and for the most part it is actively discouraged. For us a large brood of children is associated with poverty and a low standard of living, not with increased wealth through social influence or a larger labour force. In the kind of community studied by anthropologists a large family may mean more daughters to sell or more sons to work the land, but for us it means overcrowding in urban conditions and more bodies to clothe and feed on a fixed salary.

Religious rites, both Hebraic and Christian, were and are performed exclusively by men. Women are only passive participants, to be preached at. In a book on Judaism, Isidore Epstein explains woman's exclusion from active participation in religious ceremonies and duties by saying:

> The vocation of womanhood is in itself considered of a sufficient sacred character as to engage a woman's attention to the exclusion of any other religious duty which must be performed at any given time and which consequently might interfere with her special tasks.[1]

It certainly suggests that religion is an exclusively male activity, and if motherhood is meant by 'the vocation of womanhood', that men need something equally sacred to compensate for a lack of purpose. And the devout husband can look forward to a meal ready and waiting when he gets home.

The Jews may have been firmly patriarchal but they did not try to diminish the importance of sexual love. Therefore, although they required woman to be obedient, they did accord her a certain honour in her own right. There is a strict code of Judaic sexual taboos, particularly concerning menstruation, but it was left to the Essenes and early Christians to advocate total celibacy as the ideal,

[1] Isidore Epstein, *Judaism*.

even if it was unattainable for the great majority of men, who would
have to make do with marriage. This basic disapproval of sexuality
diminished the standing of women—there is no hint of the sacred
tasks of womanhood in the biting tones of St. Paul:

> Let your women keep silence in the churches; for it is not permitted
> unto them to speak; but they are commanded to be under obedience,
> as also saith the law.
> And if they will learn any thing, let them ask their husbands at
> home: for it is a shame for women to speak in the church.[1]

This prohibition has lasted down to the present day, although
by now most men are more interested in the rituals of Stock
Exchange or Parliament. Meanwhile the Church may be dying on
its feet, but it will cling to the last to the male exclusiveness which
was its *raison d'être* in the first place. There is, of course, an acute
shortage of new recruits to the clergy nowadays, faith is at a low
ebb and the financial rewards are poor, whilst few people nowadays
expect compensation in the hereafter. On 9th August 1968 the
Guardian reported on a debate amongst church dignitaries as to
whether women should be allowed into the priesthood. 'If the
Church is to be thrown open to women,' objected one archbishop,
'it will be the death knell of the appeal of the Church for men.'
Another dignitary remarked on the fact that there had been no
women amongst the Apostolic Twelve, and added: 'What we had
to ask ourselves was whether this was a haphazard sociological
phenomenon.' Of course it was no such thing. There was a
legendary Pope Joan, who like any female who dares to usurp male
power, was richly endowed with vices, lust naturally paramount;
but she finally betrayed herself by giving birth to a child during
a public procession through the streets of Rome.

As the external controls over woman in a patriarchal society
become weaker, sexual taboos are strengthened and elaborated, and
the fear of woman also becomes stronger. The fear of emasculation
may be expressed directly, as it sometimes is in the medieval
accounts of witchcraft, more often it shows itself at one remove,
like the Nyakyusa tribesman who declared: 'If I have always been

---

[1] *First Epistle to the Corinthians*, XIV, 34-5.

all right and strong and I find that I get tired walking and hoeing, I think: "What is it? See, always I was all right and now I am very tired." My friends say: "It is woman, you have lain with one who was menstruating." And if I eat food and start diarrhoea, they say: "It is women, they have committed adultery!" "[1]

The later elaborations of the Old Testament stories show a growing devaluation of sex. According to fourth- and fifth-century midrashes Adam refrained from sexual intercourse with Eve for one hundred and thirty years after the death of Abel, for fear that his next son might also be killed. As a result both he and Eve were bothered by incubi and succubi during that time, resulting in the creation of hordes of demons[2]—as always, unnatural restraints produce a result far worse than the one to be avoided, throw the Devil out of the front door and he comes back in through the window. According to an ápocryphal *Book of Adam*, preserved in an Ethiopic text of the sixth century, Adam and Eve were only taught the sins of the flesh after the Fall, since procreation had not been necessary before, and Satan—assisted by a band of fallen angels—was their teacher.[3]

In the Christian religion one finds what amounts to a total separation of spiritual and physical love, a renunciation of sexuality which is almost homosexual in its sentimental evocation of the pure mother figure and its emphasis on the union and companionship of a select band of brothers, the twelve Apostles. The writings of Christian saints are full of the struggle to overthrow the torments of the flesh, and often the repressed sexual urge took strange shapes—they saw visions, went into 'spiritual' ecstasies which they described in quite obviously sexual language, and were tormented by demons.

A more balanced, less ecstatic saint, was Augustine. He certainly knew sexual passion, and had a healthy appetite for women which he had to conquer. But the references to his mother in the *Confessions* bear a marked and interesting resemblance to our image of the Virgin Mary. She is humble and submission as patriarchy

---

[1] Mary Douglas, *Purity and Danger*, p. 133, quoting from Monica Wilson, *Rituals and Kinship among the Nyakusa.*

[2] Robert Graves & Raphael Pata, *Hebrew Myths* etc., p. 98.

[3] Ibid., p. 89.

requires, but the father figure is largely rejected—Augustine tells us that his father was an unbeliever and an adulterer. In the following passage one almost gets the impression that Augustine sees himself as Christ, fathered by God:

> For she did all that she could to see that you, my God, should be a Father to me rather than he. In this you helped her to turn the scales against her husband, whom she always obeyed because by obeying him she obeyed your law, thereby showing greater virtue than he did.[1]

Under Christianity the harsh facts of life in the Judaic patriarchy are hazed over in an aura of sentimentality and idealism. Much the same thing was to happen in the nineteenth century, when women were strongly dominated but put on a pedestal of sugary sentiment at the same time. I suppose that Saint Augustine's portrait of his mother, next to the ever-recurring image of the Virgin Mary herself, could be regarded as the most perfect description of Christian motherhood:

> In this way my mother was brought up in modesty and temperance. It was you who taught her to obey her parents rather than they who taught her to obey you, and when she was old enough, they gave her in marriage to a man she served as her lord. . . . He was unfaithful to her, but her patience was so great that his infidelity never became a cause of quarrelling between them. For she looked to you to show him mercy, hoping that chastity would come with faith. Though he was remarkably kind, he had a hot temper, but my mother knew better than to say or do anything to resist him when he was angry. If his anger was unreasonable, she used to wait until he was calm and composed and then took the opportunity of explaining what she had done. Many women, whose faces were disfigured by blows from husbands far sweeter-tempered than her own, used to gossip together and complain of the behaviour of their men-folk. My mother would meet this complaint with another—about the women's tongues. Her manner was light but her meaning serious when she told them that ever since they had heard the marriage read over them, they ought to have regarded it as a contract which bound them to serve their husbands, and from that time onward they should remember their condition and not defy their masters.[2]

[1] *Confessions* of St. Augustine (translated by R. S. Pine-Coffin), p. 32.
[2] Ibid., p. 194.

But this reverence for his mother does not extend to any woman with whom Augustine had sexual relations, and as far as one can make out from the *Confessions* he treated them rather badly. In love he was passionate, jealous, quarrelsome and totally egotistic, not uncommon faults. He also speaks disparagingly of sexual love. He suffered a good deal when he abandoned a beloved mistress in order to contract an advantageous marriage, but although he is eloquent about his own misery he shows neither guilt nor sympathy with regard to the mistress, who presumably could not have been too happy either.

Saint Augustine rationalizes his attitude on the necessary submission of woman to man as follows:

And finally we see man, made in your image and likeness, ruling over all the irrational animals for the very reason that he was made in your image and resembles you, that is, because he has the power of reason and understanding. And just as in man's soul there are two forces, one which is dominant because it deliberates and one which obeys because it is subject to such guidance, in the same way, in the physical sense, woman has been made for man. In her mind and her rational intelligence she has a nature the equal of man's, but in sex she is physically subject to him in the same way as our natural impulses need to be subjected to the reasoning power of the mind, in order that the actions to which they lead may be inspired by the principles of good conduct.[1]

Augustine seems to be trying to limit female subjection to the sexual sphere, where it was of primary importance. I suppose his great reverence for the woman who was his mother, plus a Christian idealism not shared by St. Paul and many later theologians, may have prevented Augustine from baldly declaring woman to be inferior to man, but in fact this passage expresses an attitude which was to run right through our European history. Man is reason, woman is unreason, man is more spiritual, whether in intellect or moral goodness, than woman, who is more physical, animal and sensual. Therefore man has to control woman. And it all springs from the mistaken hope that man, rational man, can control the animal side of his own nature.

[1] Ibid., p. 344.

But this is precisely what man can never do: the two aspects have to be reconciled, not set to war with each other. The more a man tries to control his lusts, the more powerful they become. It is an obvious phenomenon associated with repression: Adam refrained from satisfying his sexual appetite, and demons multiplied in the night. A small itch becomes devilish torment, what Augustine called 'hell's black river of lust'. Woman, the object of that lust, made to take the blame for the dark, uncontrollable side of man's nature, takes demonic form and becomes a witch.

A belief in magic and witchcraft obviously goes with ignorance, but superstition which is strongly associated with women rather than men, must bear some relationship to a male-dominated society, and more particularly to sexual taboos. If sex is wicked, woman must be wicked.

The evil power of woman is in the fearful imagination of man, and has little connection with what she actually tries to accomplish. Even the Trobriand Islanders believed in female witches, and Malinowski found that the basic difference between male and female sorcery was that 'the wizard actually carries on his trade, while the witch's activities exist only in the folk-lore and in the imagination of the native'.[1] The powers ascribed to female witches were much more impressive than those attributed to their male counterparts—a witch was supposed to be able to fly through the night, change herself into a firefly, a night bird or a flying fox, was said to feed on corpses and have sexual intercourse with evil spirits, who brought diseases and instructed the witch in the art of doing harm. A male sorcerer's art, on the other hand, was much more concrete, almost amounted to a rational system, and his supernatural powers were very restricted.

The powers of these Polynesian witches are similar to those which were ascribed to witches from pre-Christian times all over Europe. But the punitive element was missing, and this is something almost unique to the Hebraic and later Christian tradition on such a large scale, though the Romans had heavy punishments for the practice of magic, including death by crucifixion or by being thrown to the beasts. Caligula's insanity was attributed to drugs

[1] Malinowski, *The Sexual Life of Savages.*

administered by his wife, Caesonia, who was put to death when he
was assassinated. The superstitious Romans also believed in old
hags who flew through the air at night, who could blight harvests
and turn their victims into animals.

Under early Salic law the official penalties for witchcraft were not
very severe, although some people accused of witchcraft undoubtedly did come to a violent end. Rabbinical Judaism, on the
other hand, relentlessly enforced the Mosaic law 'Thou shalt not
suffer a witch to live', and mass executions on a large scale were
carried out. But the persecution of a veritable epidemic of witchcraft which began to spread across the whole of Christian Europe
towards the end of the fourteenth century is a very strange phenomenon. Witch trials could be either secular or conducted by the
Church, and the methods of the Inquisition—which extracted confessions by torture and disallowed defence counsels and appeals—
were ideally suited to producing two witches where there had only
been one before. Perhaps one of the most notorious cases which
has come down to us through historical records is that of the
witches of Arras in the fifteenth century, when witches were being
tried and burned all over Europe. One extorted confession in the
town of Langres ultimately implicated the whole of the citizenry
of Arras, as each confession led to another, and there was a distinct
possibility of many other districts of France becoming implicated
before the Duke of Burgundy intervened. Ultimately good names
were restored, and an inquisitor was actually brought to trial
(uniquely) before a lay court, but before that the whole town had
been thrown into a panic, with trade and industry disrupted, and
no man's credit good since he might be arrested and his property
confiscated at any time.

The epidemic spread like wildfire, fed by religious zeal, superstitious fear and, often, political or other motives of self-interest.
It even reached remote Ireland, where Lady Alice Kyteler of
Kilkenny was accused, in 1325, of having killed four husbands by
sorcery. The accusers were the children by the last three husbands,
who had not inherited. Lady Alice escaped to England but confessions were elicited with a whip from her accomplices. Thus
Petronilla, one of her maids, confessed after six whippings that she

had been the intermediary between Lady Alice and her demon lover (who had two companions, black as Ethiopians), that they had sacrificed cocks at the crossroads and that they had concocted potions from the brains of an unbaptized child, with herbs and worms, in the skull of a beheaded robber. The unfortunate Petronilla was burned, as were others involved.[1]

Berne, Como, Heidelberg, Toulouse, all had major witch trials, and the fires burned. As the minds of the people became more and more familiar with the idea that witches were anywhere and everywhere, that they could account for cattle diseases, failed crops, a sick child or simply illicit passion which disturbed monastic or matrimonial harmony, the accusations became more frequent, and a visiting inquisitor—far from having to hunt out his witches—would be inundated with accusations, making his task an easy one. Thus, for example, an inquisitor's visit to Como in 1485 resulted in forty-one witches burned in one small district of the Grisons.

The Papal Bull of Pope Innocent VIII in 1484 gave a special impetus to the hunting out of witches. 'It has come to our ears,' he wrote, 'that numbers of both sexes do not avoid to have intercourse with demons, Incubi and Succubi; and that by their sorceries, and by their incantations, charms, and conjurations, they suffocate, extinguish, and cause to perish the births of women, the increase of animals, the corn of the ground, the grapes of the vineyard and the fruit of the trees, as well as men, women, flocks, herds, and other various kinds of animals, vines and apple trees, grass, corn and other fruits of the earth; making and procuring that men and women, flocks and herds and other animals shall suffer and be tormented both from within and without, so that men beget not, nor women conceive; and they impede the conjugal action of men and women.'[2]

The impetus was terrible—while Sprenger and Institoris became the scourge of Germany (in one small town they burned forty-eight people within five years) Brescia burned seventy men and seventy women in 1510, and three hundred were burned at Como in 1514. 'In the madness of the hour it was currently reported that on the

[1] Henry Charles Lea, *A History of the Inquisition*, Vol. 3, p. 519.
[2] Margaret A. Murray, *The Witch-Cult in Western Europe*, p. 24.

60

plain of Tonale, near Brescia, the customary gathering of the Sabbat exceeded twenty-five thousand souls; and in 1518 the Senate was officially informed that the inquisitor had burned seventy witches of the Valcamonica, that he had as many in his prisons, and that those suspected or accused amounted to about five thousand, or one fourth of the inhabitants of the valleys. It was time to interfere, and the Signoria interposed effectually, leading to violent remonstrances from Rome.'[1] England, not subject to the Roman Catholic Inquisition, reached its witch-hunting peak somewhat later than the rest of Europe. In 1325 twenty-eight persons were brought to trial, accused of trying to bring about the death of Edward II with the help of sorcerers, but ordinary jury trial led to their acquittal; as late as 1372 a man accused of sorcery was discharged, since English secular courts did not extract confessions by torture. But in 1407 Henry IV issued letters to his bishops warning them against the horrors of the agents of Satan and commissioning them to imprison them with or without trial. James VI of Scotland, later James I of England, wrote a book against witchcraft, and it is perhaps due to his influence that witches were tried and executed in the 1590s in North Berwick and Aberdeen, and the well-known Lancashire witches were put on trial in 1613. In fact the epidemic of witches does not appear to have reached its peak in England until the seventeenth century, and the punitive impetus was strongly puritanical. However, English witches did escape being burned alive, which was a French refinement, and were usually hung. How far, in fact, the women of Somerset, Huntingdonshire and most of the other counties of England and Scotland actually did practise some form of witchcraft is a matter for dispute. Margaret Murray argues that, since English courts did not extract confessions by physical torture, the confessions must have been genuine. On the other hand the tests used for proving someone a witch were hardly designed to give anyone a fair chance.

Although a large number of men were tried for sorcery, on the whole witch-hunting and a belief in witchcraft is overwhelmingly associated with women. The fear of her occult or supernatural powers tends to be in inverse proportion to her actual power. From

[1] Henry Charles Lea, *A History of the Inquisition*, Vol. 3, p. 547.

time to time theologians were somewhat bothered by the fact that witches with such extraordinary powers should be quite unable to save themselves from arrest and execution, and this was explained by saying that they lost their powers the moment they were put under arrest and could do nothing against inquisitors or officers of the law. Not only is witchcraft primarily associated with women, but the connotations are primarily sexual. There is always great emphasis on witches having intercourse with the Devil, on obscene orgies, on animal 'familiars', and apart from the damage to property most of the harm done by witchcraft is of a sexual nature. Considered in this light one can perhaps regard large-scale witch-hunting as the Christian Church's last desperate attempt to conquer the Devil in man himself—sexuality in the shape of woman. The Church went under and the Devil survived triumphant.

This interpretation of the witchcraft phenomenon is confirmed by an examination of *Malleus Maleficarum* ('Hammer of Witches'), written by the witchcraft inquisitor Jacob Sprenger. Published shortly after the Papal Bull of 1484, it was the definitive book on the subject of witchcraft, and the reason why witches should be so much more numerous than wizards is examined and explained at great length. Although there are a few good women, declares Sprenger, all the more precious for their extreme rarity, the great majority of women are in league with the Devil and constitute a threat to man. The reader is left in no doubt about which part of the anatomy is in danger. 'The power of the devil lies in the privy parts of men.'

> ... although the devil cannot directly operate upon the understanding and will of man, yet . . . he can act upon the body, or upon the faculties belonging to or allied to the body, whether they be inner or outer perceptions.

Woman is a useful tool for the Devil because she acts as a kind of intermediary, working on man's body. The dangers of contact are emphasized:

> . . . the devil cannot so easily and readily do harm by himself to mankind, as he can harm them through the instrumentality of witches, although they are his servants. In the first place we may consider the act of generation. But for every act which has an effect

upon another some kind of contact must be established, and because the devil, who is a spirit, can have no such actual contact with a human body, since there is nothing common of this between them, therefore he uses some human instruments, and upon these he bestows the power of hurting by bodily touch.

Sprenger has no lack of causes to explain the link between woman and the powers of darkness. She is 'feebler in mind and body' and 'naturally more impressionable, and more ready to receive the influence of a disembodied spirit'. Women are also more liable to waver from true religion, have 'weak memories', and 'it is a natural vice in them not to be disciplined, but to follow their own impulses without any sense of what is due'. The female of the species is also 'a liar by nature', vindictive, malicious, quick to seek vengeance when scorned or abandoned by a male, and is incapable of keeping a secret, once she has found it out by evil arts. All faults attributed by Milton to Delilah. In short, 'without the wickedness of women . . . the world would still remain proof against innumerable dangers'. Unfortunately for males not on their guard, the wicked creature has the sweet voice of a siren, luring men to their doom, and all her thoughts are turned to the art of pleasing men.

But the core of woman's natural viciousness, says Sprenger, lies in her insatiable lust, and it is her dreadful and perpetual appetite that allows her to copulate with the Devil. 'The natural reason is that she is more carnal than a man, as is clear from her many carnal abominations.' This inherent flaw (among so many) can be explained by the fact that 'there was a defect in the formation of the first woman, since she was formed from a bent rib, that is, a rib of the breast, which is bent as it were in a contrary direction to a man. And since through this defect she is an imperfect animal, she always deceives'. And since hell has no fury like a woman scorned, the man who tries to break off a relationship once it has begun is in dire peril:

> . . . just as through the first defect in their intelligence they are more prone to abjure the faith; so through their second defect of inordinate affections and passions they search for, brood over, and inflict various vengeances, either by witchcraft, or by some other means. Wherefore it is no wonder that so great a number of witches exist in this sex.

Woman, as Freud was to say four hundred years later, is hostile to the demands of civilization, or, in Sprenger's words: 'If we inquire, we find that nearly all the kingdoms of the world have been overthrown by women', and he quotes Helen of Troy, Jezebel, and Cleopatra. There is a fine Biblical ring to his words of warning:

> ... woman is a wheedling and secret enemy. And that she is more perilous than a snare does not speak of the snare of hunters, but of devils. For men are caught not only through their carnal desires, when they see and hear women: For S. Bernard says: Their face is as a burning wind, and their voice the hissing of serpents: but they also cast wicked spells on countless men and animals. And when it is said that her heart is a net, it speaks of the inscrutable malice which reigns in their hearts. And her hands are as bands for binding, for when they place their hands on a creature to bewitch it, then with the help of the devil they perform their design. To conclude. All witchcraft comes from carnal lust, which is in women insatiable.

The fact is that for Sprenger witches and women are synonymous, and his vituperative remarks are intended to embrace the whole of womankind. He must have enjoyed his work as a witchhunter, which would really only have come to an end once the whole sex was wiped out.

The most awful and constantly emphasized results of such dangerous sexual contact with women, i.e. witches, are all damage of a sexual kind, and include venereal diseases, sterility, impotence, and a sort of phantasmal castration. Impotence with a particular woman, quarrels with one's lawful spouse or a lack of desire to have intercourse with her, a consuming passion for another woman outside the marriage, all these are put down to witchcraft—understandably, since faithful and monogamous marriage was the only form of sexuality condoned by the Church. But the Old Devil was hard to put down. Castration was somewhat more tricky: Sprenger maintained that it was not possible for a witch actually to remove a man's genitals, but she could make them invisible both to the unfortunate victim himself and to any bystander. For example, a young man had an intrigue with a girl, and when he abandoned her he lost his member, 'that is to say, some glamour was cast over it so that he could see or touch nothing but his smooth body'. The young man went to drown his sorrows in a tavern, where a woman advised him to return to the witch and ask her to restore him to health. The young man followed this advice, and when the witch protested her innocence he half strangled her with a towel. Under the threat of death the woman touched him between the thighs with her hand, saying: 'Now you have what you desire.'

> And the young man, as he afterwards said, plainly felt, before he verified it by looking or touching, that his member had been restored to him by the mere touch of the witch.

Such is the nature of witchcraft.

Since the Church condoned holy matrimony for the purposes of procreation, Sprenger is particularly vehement against the way the Devil uses witches to upset the stability of marriage. The act against witchcraft introduced by James I made 'the intent to provoke any person to unlawfull love punishable by imprisonment and the pillory at the first offence, by death on the second'.

Since Sprenger considered that all women were either practising or potential witches, and thus instruments of the Devil, he is led to a curious conclusion—that Christ the Redeemer descended from Heaven only to save the male sex. Having stated that 'all witchcraft comes from carnal lust, which is in women insatiable', he goes on:

> Wherefore for the sake of fulfilling their lusts they consort even with devils. . . . And blessed be the Highest Who has so far preserved the male sex from so great a crime: for since He was willing to be born and to suffer for us, therefore He has granted men this privilege.

Truly, one can say, a religion created by men, for men.

III

Mammon

As God, so Mammon. Man's wish to control woman arose out of his desire to cheat death by founding a male line. Establishing the importance of that line by the accumulation of power and property, he increased his own importance. Ironically, it was through the accumulation of property, the ability to acquire wealth, that his domination—in the modern sense that we understand through our more recent history—was re-established and confirmed after God lost his immediacy and became less real.

'When Adam delved and Eve span/Who was then the gentleman?' goes the old rhyme, and the question is pertinent enough in a culture that has not reached a complex state of development. In a simple, fairly primitive society the social set-up may allow a man to exert a certain amount of physical control over his womenfolk, and in so far as this physical control is inadequate he will evolve a system of sexual taboos, and emphasize his authority through religion, but his basic problem is survival, and to achieve this end the combined efforts of man and woman are equally required. Men, women and even children have an important part to play, and must perform vital everyday tasks. Although it may be true that, as Margaret Mead says, whatever tasks are assigned to the menfolk of the community are by common consent considered more important, the fact remains that all tasks are essential, and everyone knows it. Perhaps it is the very assurance of this fact that makes it possible for women to concede prestige gracefully to men—because they know quite well that the tasks they perform are just as vital. The survival of a primitive community is always at risk—the next meal has to be found, the hut may collapse, disease

66

may strike, and there is no organized insurance against disaster. When a community is struggling to survive the co-operation of everyone is important. We see an analogy in more civilized societies in the fact that during wars women suddenly cease to be redundant —thus Florence Nightingale could make nursing a suitable profession for women during the Crimean War, whilst the unemancipated woman who had been chaining herself to park railings prior to the First World War in the fight for rights suddenly found herself working in munitions factories, after which no one seriously disputed her right to vote.

When Adam delved and Eve span. . . . But a time came when Adam could hire a man to delve for him. The rise of capitalism is the root cause of the modern social and economic discrimination against women, which came to a peak in the last century. It was in the prosperous middle classes that the problems of the dependent woman were felt most acutely in the nineteenth century, and it was this *bourgeoisie* that developed with capitalism in the seventeenth century. In the working class, meanwhile, women became the cheapest form of labour.

The men who defended what they considered to be their inalienable rights with such vigour and conviction during the last century were not aware that some of these privileges were in fact of comparatively recent date, and that the sharp division of roles— with woman staying at home and man leaving the home to work for financial reward that would maintain both of them—was a comparatively recent development.

It has often been argued that female discontent with her womanly lot ill becomes her, and that when a woman accepts her subjection gracefully both she and man are much the happier for it. 'Look at Shakespeare's heroines,' is quoted as an example, 'there is nothing meek or submissive about them, and yet you never hear one of them airing feminist grievances.' No, because in spite of the limitations that undoubtedly existed for a woman as compared to a man, the restrictions were not nearly so suffocating and intolerable as they were later to become.

Shakespeare's day was the period of England's renaissance. The Dark Ages were well and truly finished with, and acquisitive

Puritanism had not yet got a strong hold. Life was still harsh and brutal but pleasure was important, and learning and artistic skills were prized by the privileged few.

Woman shared in the prosperous heyday, and no doubt her social position was aided by the fact that England was ruled by a strong queen, unaided by a male consort. Elizabeth's determined refusal to allow any private passions to infringe on her royal authority certainly contradicts the image of the dependent little woman leaning heavily on the arm of her man.

The fear of God waned with the power of the Church, and the connotations between the fires of hell, sexual temptation and female wickedness were no longer so powerful. Later Puritanism was to reinforce sexual taboos, not for the sake of eternal salvation, but for more effective concentration on the business of acquiring wealth. There was a change in the view of marriage at about this time. Under Roman Catholicism it was regarded as essentially a holy sacrament, with Protestantism it became primarily a civil contract.

One must not paint too rosy a picture of the Elizabethan woman's existence. Her upbringing was rather on the spartan side, and she was certainly expected to obey, first her parents, and later her husband, to be loving and submissive, and not to leave her home unaccompanied by her husband, unless she was going to church or on some charitable errand. Although her duties were primarily domestic, the manuals of the time make it clear that it was thought good for her to have an education in the arts, literature, music, and, since the Elizabethans were meticulous about domestic book-keeping, mathematics. Although corporal punishment was still permissible it was not really approved of, and husbands were advised to enforce their will through love rather than blows.[1]

Marriage was considered a form of lifelong partnership and friendship. The Elizabethan wife was very far from being kept in enforced idleness, since running a household meant providing most of the things that the members of the household needed—linen, clothes, food and medicines. Wives often managed large estates whilst their husbands were away at court or fighting. Frederick,

[1] See Carroll Camden, *The Elizabethan Woman*.

68

Duke of Württemberg, visited England in 1602 and wrote that 'the women have much more liberty than perhaps in any other place' and there was a proverb abroad which ran: 'England is a paradise for women, a prison for servants, and a hell or purgatory for horses.'

One can argue how far the breakaway from Roman Catholicism and the influence of Elizabeth were responsible for the relatively favourable position of women compared to the rest of Europe at that time, but they are highly important in my opinion. Certainly James I, coming as he did from the puritanical wilds of Scotland, where John Knox had enveighed against the monstrous regiment of women, helped to reverse the trend. James was a firm believer in witchcraft, wrote a book about it because he was so angered at appeals for moderation in the treatment of witches, and in 1590 the witches of North Berwick were tried (with the use of torture) for attempting to bring about the death of James I and his queen by witchcraft, first by raising a storm which nearly succeeded in wrecking the queen's ship between Denmark and Scotland, and later by melting a wax image. It follows as no surprise that James should have taken a thoroughly conservative attitude with regard to female subordination. When a learned young lady was presented at court, and her knowledge of Latin, Greek and Hebrew were praised, James is said to have replied: 'But can she spin?' In 1620 he became annoyed at female presumption in adopting male dress (the offence which finally sent the witch Joan of Arc to the stake!) and urged the clergy to take the matter in hand, and 'to inveigh vehemently against the insolence of our women, and theyre wearing of brode brimed hats, pointed dublets, theyre hayre cut short or shorne'. The popularity of Swetnam's *The Arraignment of Lewd, Idle, Froward and Unconstant Women*, which was published in 1615 and went into numerous editions, is some indication of the change of climate after the death of Elizabeth.

In medieval and Elizabethan times there was little physical or psychological division between the idea of 'home' and that of 'work', nor the sharp division between male and female roles that has come about as a result. The merchant lived above his shop, the craftsman's workshop was also the place where he lived. Although during the reign of Elizabeth the enclosure movement was well under way and capitalism was already being applied to industry, it was still largely a society of small craftsmen. The household was a working, productive unit, and the wife's labour was very necessary to her husband—she saw to the accounts, performed tasks in the productive process which did not require maximum muscular strength, and she and her maidservants fed the journeymen and kept a watchful and motherly eye on the young apprentices. Each man would expect to become a master craftsman sooner or later, and it was only during the learning period that he worked in the establishment of another man. It was the kind of marital partnership that has really only survived in one or two spheres—on the smallholding, for instance, where the wife looks after the poultry and the butter production; in the country pub where husband and wife both serve behind the bar and the wife perhaps provides meals as well. A way of life, in fact, that can only survive when the place of work and domestic quarters are situated in the same place.

That a craftsman's wife was considered an important partner in his work is confirmed by her position in the gilds. As his helpmate, she was usually free of his gild, and would carry on the business after her husband's death. It was normal for wives to inherit a business, rather than for the business to pass into the control of the sons of the family, and widows of master craftsmen were much sought after in marriage as a way of entry into a specialized trade, such as printing. The wife of a craftsman or merchant would also supervise the organization of domestic chores, carried out largely by servants, and these chores themselves amounted to a small industry, and were more productive and demanding than anything we mean by the phrase nowadays. Bread was baked, butter and cheese made, ale brewed, thread spun, linen woven and bleached, clothes cut and sewn. Nowadays if a woman bakes her own bread or cakes and knits sweaters for the family it is an individual fad or hobby, but it is not essential because the needs can be supplied from other sources at little or no extra cost. But in those days the comfort and welfare of everyone depended very largely on woman's work, and she had no cause to complain that she 'worked all day and there was nothing to show for it', or that her life consisted in cleaning up after other people.

It was not only usual for a widow to carry on the family business rather than for that business to be sold or taken over by a son, it was also quite normal for a married woman to engage in business on her own account. The Customs of the City of London, for instance, declared that: 'Where a woman coverte de baron follows any craft within the said city to herself apart, with which the husband in no way intermeddles, such woman shall be bound as a single woman in all that concerns her said craft. And if the wife shall plead as a single woman in a Court of Record, she shall have her law and other advantages by way of plea just as a single woman. And if she is condemned she shall be committed to prison until she shall have made satisfaction; and neither the husband nor his goods shall in such case be charged or interfered with.' (*Liber Albus,* 1419.) And most other boroughs took the same line on married women independently engaged in trade. A petition that silk weavers presented to Henry VI in 1455 shows clearly the medieval attitude to women's work, that 'it is pleasyng to God that all his Creatures be set in vertueux occupation and labour accordyng to their degrees'. The petitioners asked for the import of silk goods to be prohibited, because 'before this tyme, many a wurshipfull woman within the seid Citee have lyved full hounourably, and therwith many good Housholds kept' and the petitioners assumed that 'Every wele disposed persone of this land, by reason and naturall favour, wold rather that wymmen of their nation born and owen blode hadde the occupation thereof, than strange people of oyer landes'. The petition was granted.[1]

The feudal peasant farmer disappeared with land enclosure and became entirely dependent on wages. With the growth of capitalism, involving more highly organized industry and the purchase of expensive machinery, many journeymen never became masters; all their lives they worked for an employer as wage-earners, which meant that the womenfolk of their household either had to follow an occupation of their own, one which could be combined with the inescapable domestic duties, or they became totally dependent on

[1] Alice Clark, *Working Life of Women in the Seventeenth Century.*

the husband and father's wage. In many cases, particularly if trade was booming under the new, more efficient conditions, the family wage brought home by the husband was adequate, and journeymen were able to form their own protective organizations; but if times were bad or there was no male breadwinner a woman had to resort to ill-paid cottage industry, like spinning, since she was tied to the home. Later, with the growth of industrial cities, the working woman of the nineteenth century would be working in the later equivalent of the cottage industry—the sweat shops that made such items as lace and shirts and straw hats, sweat shops that evaded the Factory Acts. In the seventeenth century a woman who had to spin anyway for her own family could make useful pin money by spinning, but a woman could barely support herself, let alone dependants, on spinning, and if there was no husband to bring in a wage she invariably became a pauper. (Wool spinning, a highly specialized skill, was an exception.) We find this situation to a large extent repeated today: many women with a husband and children are able to earn enough money for 'extras', but become destitute and need state assistance if the male, the main breadwinner, disappears.

The changing situation was reflected in the gilds, and women were gradually ousted from them. In some cases, as in weaving, the reason given was that women were not strong enough to handle the more modern, heavier machinery. Ironically, Karl Marx saw mechanization as a major cause of the exploitation of women's labour, since machines made muscle power unnecessary! The real reason for the exploitation of women's labour during the industrial revolution was, of course, quite simply that it was cheaper. Nowadays unequal pay is usually justified by the claim that the work produced is unequal, but it would hardly have suited the hard-headed industrialists of the past to employ women in preference to men if their work had not been equal value for less money. If it had been simply less value for less money, they would probably have taken on male labour in many cases, since the fact that women's labour was cheaper often resulted in whole communities of men being unemployed, taking the working wife's place and looking after the children. Ever since the rise of capitalism we have had the sex-role division of woman at home, man at work, but in practice it was only the upper and middle classes, who could ever live up to what was essentially an 'ideal' of the new *bourgeoisie*. Lower down the social scale the official line that 'woman does not work' has always provided an undercurrent of cheap, because 'unofficial' work, and in a *laissez-faire* situation the employer can play off second-class labour against first-class labour, to the detriment of both, although the first-class labourer imagines himself to be acting in his own interest by taking a protective, exclusive stance, whether through gilds or trade unions. His behaviour is doubly short-sighted when one considers that, taken all in all, the members of one group or married to the members of the other group—and yet they allow themselves to be played off against each other! The undercurrent of cheap female labour still exists today—a recent report shows that more than half Britain's eight million working women earn less than five shillings an hour, and that only 4 per cent can expect to earn as much as ten shillings an hour.

Meanwhile the capitalist's wife was becoming a domesticated and idle plaything. Unlike the small craftsman, the capitalist employer did not need the services of his wife in the workshop or to do the book-keeping. He had money, machinery and permanent employees to keep all aspects of the business running efficiently. It was an element in his social status that his wife should be kept in elegant idleness, a sexual plaything, adorned with the fine clothes and jewels that he could afford to buy her. Compare Shakespeare's heroine to the ladies of Restoration comedy and you see the change that has taken place in under a century. Shakespeare's heroines are strong, full of life and wit, passionate in love and resourceful in adversity and in the defence of those they love. 'It is remarkable that Shakespeare's women almost always *make love*,' wrote George Eliot in her commonplace book, 'in opposition to the conventional notion of what is fitting for woman.' They are women who actively control their own destinies, and there is nothing passive or limited about them. But the ladies of Restoration comedy spend their days paying social calls, vacillating between amorous intrigue and an attack of the vapours. They put on airs and graces, flirt and talk about love without appearing to feel much, and the overriding impression one gets is that both they and the gentlemen they dally with appear to be trying desperately to fend off encroaching boredom, no doubt the result of too much leisure bought by wealth. Serious conversation is not *de rigueur*, and by the time we get to Sheridan the ladies have become sentimental too, and spend their time reading silly novels of romance, in contrast to the studied cynicism of their predecessors. Pepys understood that it was 'want of worke' and the loneliness of her position which made his spouse so ill-tempered, and liable to complain about the mess he made in the house. 'It is fit the wretch should have something to content herself with,' he remarked on the subject of her jewellery. An affectation to learning was looked down on in a woman and could seriously damage a girl's prospects of matrimony—Molière in France made fun of the *précieuses ridicules* and *femmes savantes* who thought they could compete with men in the sphere of learning. In the eighteenth century Lady Mary Wortley Montagu was to advise girls to learn but to hide their knowledge as though it was some dreadful disease to be ashamed of. When she advised that her granddaughter should be taught history, geography, languages and philosophy, her daughter complained that such an education for a girl would cost too much—and this from a member of the aristocracy.

The discrepancy between male and female education was also becoming an increasingly important factor—if only because education was becoming a practical necessity rather than a rather useless veneer. Education is a form of investment, and if a woman is destined to be either a housekeeper, or a lady of leisure, or a source of cheap and unskilled labour, there is no point in wasting on her the long education that increasing specialization involves. Take medicine, for example. In the Middle Ages there were women studying medicine and law at Bologna, and a French edict of 1311 specifying tests for doctors mentions both men and women, and in the same century Frankfurt numbered fifteen women amongst those who had studied and practised medicine.[1] But in fact every medieval lady prepared her own cures, ointments and plague water, and village women who prepared love potions or charmed away warts were to provide the raw material for witch-hunting.

[1] See Evelyne Sullerot, *Histoire et sociologie du travail feminin.*

Mammon

Specialized as it is, modern medicine as we know it is in fact a very new science, and even in the seventeenth century a rough and ready medicine was practised by both men and women. It was results that mattered, not qualifications, and with so much ignorance and quackery common sense might get better results than academic learning. The account books of boroughs and parishes in the seventeenth century show that the poor were treated medically and surgically by both men and women, but as medicine became more scientific and subject to government and professional control this changed, and even midwifery, a function traditionally associated with women since time immemorial, began to require an education from which women were excluded. Male midwives appeared, or doctors insisted on being consulted during childbirth.

This growing division between the sphere of work and that of home—both physical and psychological—not only created a situation where the woman became an economic dependant, but meant that a wife no longer understood her husband's work, his problems and preoccupations, she could no longer keep up with him; the husband, on the other hand, had less constant contact with his family, and tended only to see his wife and children during the hours reserved for leisure—his central preoccupation was with the business of making money. Nevertheless, although he might be a remote figure his authority was supreme, because the whole family now relied on his earnings. Whatever his wife contributed within the home must remain secondary.

Marriage was no longer a holy sacrament, it was a civil contract which, for those who had it, protected private property and inheritance. I began by saying that man's interest in the domination of woman stems from his desire to achieve a kind of immortality through his children, particularly his sons, to whom he can then hand down the wealth he has accumulated. Wealthy fathers with only a daughter to marry off would give a handsome dowry, but in return required that the groom's estate should be entailed on 'their' first grandson. Wortley Montagu's refusal to do this nearly ruined Lady Mary's chances of marrying the man of her own choice. Wortley, still tempted by her beautiful eyes and even more handsome dowry, gave his opinions on the subject to his friend

Richard Steele, who wrote an essay in the *Tatler* in which Isaac Bickerstaff discusses mercenary marriages (12th September 1710). The suitor declares that 'in full and perfect health of body, and a sound mind, not knowing which of my children will prove better or worse, I give to my firstborn, be he perverse, ungrateful, impious, or cruel, the lump and bulk of my estate . . . hereby further confessing and covenanting that I am from henceforth married, and dead in law'.[1] And what did a girl have to gain from such a match, romantic expectations apart? Freedom from parental authority, social status, and enough pin money written into the marriage contract to make life tolerably pleasurable. It is important to remember that, although we may regard marriage with dependence as a form of slavery, for the women of the past it was regarded as the only possible form of freedom—it was only through marriage that she could become a woman in her own right in the eyes of the world, and much depended on finding a tolerable and reasonably tolerant mate. The tone of cynicism which pervades discussions of love and marriage in letters and literature during the seventeenth and eighteenth centuries is fully justified—money had become much more important than religion, and people were very well aware of what they were doing in marriage—ensuring the future wealth of their families, getting themselves safely married and making the most of life afterwards. No one really expected a wife to remain faithful, the renewed emphasis on female virtue was really part of the romantic revolution, which was a reaction from worldly cynicism.

But female virtue is of course necessary to ensure that the son to whom a man passes on his wealth is really his own son, and not a cuckoo in the nest. This fact alone made the romantic revolution necessary, once the religious sexual taboos were no longer taken all that seriously. With God firmly superseded by Mammon the property motive becomes much more explicit in the justification of a double standard of morality. Thus we have Rousseau, the father of the romantic revolution himself, the man who also advocated political revolution on the grounds that excessive and unequal property is unjust, writing:

[1] Robert Halsband, *The Life of Lady Mary Wortley Montagu*, p. 15.

Mammon

Women do wrong to complain of the inequality of man-made laws; this inequality is not of man's making, or at any rate it is not the result of mere prejudice, but of reason. She to whom nature has entrusted the care of the children must hold herself responsible for them to their father. No doubt every breach of faith is wrong, and every faithless husband, who robs his wife of the sole reward of the stern duties of her sex, is cruel and unjust; but the faithless wife is worse; she destroys the family and breaks the bonds of nature; when she gives her husband children who are not his own, she is false both to him and them, her crime is not infidelity but treason. To my mind, it is the source of dissension and of crime of every kind. Can any position be more wretched than that of the unhappy father who, when he clasps his child to his breast, is haunted by the suspicion that this is the child of another, the badge of his own dishonour, a thief who is robbing his own children of their inheritance.[1]

It is a man and 'his' children that are important, not a man and his wife and children. Once the process of industrialization had made man the sole breadwinner, given him the economic control of wealth, one sees over and over again that he regards this wealth as solely his—his wife has not 'earned' it, therefore she has no right to enjoy it. Thus Schopenhauer, recommending that inheritance should go through male descendants only, wrote:

> That widows burn themselves on the corpse of their husbands is indeed shocking, but that they should spend the fortune which the husband, consoling himself that he was working for his children, had acquired by the steady industry of his whole life, with their lovers, is also shocking.[2]

That a wife should outlive her husband is intolerable enough, but that she should survive to enjoy dissipating his immortality, the symbol of his potency, is intolerable.

The desire for some form of immortality is fundamental to the whole issue, otherwise why should the fear that one's child is not actually one's own be so haunting, terrible enough, in Strindberg's view, to drive a man insane. He also explores the theme in his autobiographical novel, *The Confession of a Fool*, and provides an answer:

> I doubted the legitimacy of my children; I was haunted by the

---

[1] *Emile*.   [2] Essay, 'On Women'.

suspicion that although they bore my name and were supported by my earnings, they were yet not my children. Nevertheless I loved them, for they had come into my life as a pledge of my future existence. Deprived of the hope to live again in my children, I floated in mid-air, like a poor phantom, breathing through roots which were not my own.[1]

The fact that all children are inevitably the product of a man and woman, that a man may bear little or no resemblance to his actual father, is customarily ignored. After all, each human being should be a human being in his or her own right, not an extension of the parent, but if the question of a vicarious immortality arises at all the mother has as much right to be perpetuated into the future as the father. But males in a patriarchal society always ignore this, just as the patriarchs of the Old Testament, in discarding a barren wife, disregarded the fact that her failure to bear children might be due to her husband's inability to give her one, and that his possible sterility should have given her a right to try elsewhere, since *he* might be depriving *her* of the inalienable right to have children and be fruitful. But no, for the ancient Hebrews woman was merely a vessel for the male seed. Similarly, Schopenhauer[2] says that 'women exist solely for the propagation of the race', somehow forgetting or ignoring the fact that women are also part of the race, and that 50 per cent of all the human beings born are female. After all, one could just as well argue that men merely exist for the impregnation of women, after which they can be gobbled up like male spiders. The idea that bearing children is the primary reason for a woman's existence has always been very widespread and is still with us. One could almost say that it is a fundamental tenet of the male mind.

With the disappearance of religious belief the idea of an immortal soul and a hereafter in some sort of heaven recedes, and this makes immortality through one's children, or through one's work or achievement, doubly important. Achievement could be expressed in accumulated wealth, or it could be intellectual achievement— also a masculine prerogative. But the concept of 'genius' is as intangible as a man's fatherhood, and the assurance of one's own cleverness is easily undermined by a questioning insecurity. The

---

[1] August Strindberg, *The Confession of a Fool.*   [2] 'On Women'.

men who put the greatest emphasis on mind as a way of bolstering their own sense of identity, men who—on the surface at least— seem very sure of their own genius and tend to regard their own qualities of mind as part of their maleness, men who look on intellect as a male prerogative and associate women with a physicality they attempt to renounce, tend also to be the greatest misogynists—Milton, Strindberg, Schopenhauer are examples.

The double standard as a way of ensuring paternity was rigorously enforced, not just by sexual taboos and a code of morality, but by law. The Matrimonial Causes Act of 1857 made adultery sufficient cause for a man to divorce his wife, but a woman was required to prove a second cause, such as desertion, cruelty, rape, incest, sodomy or bestiality, in order to obtain a divorce from her husband. During the debate on this bill the Lord Chancellor said that 'the adultery of the wife might be the means of palming spurious offspring upon the husband'.

'The steady industry of his whole life,' wrote Schopenhauer in all seriousness, and the sentiment comes oddly from him. It shows how deeply the idea of money-making as a virtue had seeped into the general consciousness. Industry and thrift became cardinal virtues with the rise of capitalism, and from now on man's prime duty was to help himself rather than his neighbour. And they are male virtues—woman, no longer being a breadwinner, represents sloth and pleasure, and the temptation to spend, which by the nineteenth century had actually become the vernacular word for ejaculation. Naturally from now on every woman would have her price—the price of virtue was simply higher than that of vice.

That God helps those who help themselves was perhaps the key maxim of the Puritans. Puritanism was the religion of the new middle class that emerged with the growth of capitalism. It put great emphasis on industry and thrift, and was equally concerned with the control of pleasure and sensuality. Naturally, pleasure (which involved spending rather than keeping) interfered with industry, and with the basic concept of capitalism that a penny not spent becomes two pennies quite rapidly. Love was considered good in so far as it stabilized marriage and the family, and was founded on reason, but passion was bad. Not, as in the old days, because the lusts of the flesh separated man from his higher nature, God, and put him in the power of his animal nature, the Devil, but because it distracted him from his God-given task of making money and improving his own position. The Puritan *bourgeois* was the first 'self-made man', and he was self-righteously proud of it. The fixed social order of medieval times, where each man lived out his life according to his degree in a pattern worked out by God, had disappeared, and now you either went up or down, and if you went down in the social scale it was largely your own fault. It was a man's sacred duty to improve his lot by his own hard work and ability, that was what God had put him in the world to do. Paupers became the object of contempt rather than of charity and pity. Being a self-made man the Puritan naturally believed in the concepts of free will, free enterprise, and the dictates of his private conscience, which became the main channel through which the Almighty spoke to him.

It follows that, just as a man's ability to make more money than his neighbour will increase his own sense of self-esteem, a man's increasing tendency to become the sole breadwinner for the family would bolster his sense of masculine superiority. Self-esteem amounting to smugness is the keynote in the words of the Angel Raphael, warning Adam to remain master over Eve in *Paradise Lost*:

> *For what admir'st thou, what transports thee so,*
> *An outside? fair no doubt, and worthy well*
> *Thy cherishing, thy honouring, and thy love,*
> *Not thy subjection: weigh with her thy self;*
> *Then value: Oft times nothing profits more*
> *Than self-esteem, grounded on just and right*
> *Well manag'd; of that skill the more thou know'st,*
> *The more she will acknowledge thee her Head,*
> *And to realities yield all her shows. . . .*[1]

The very vocabulary seems to belong to a merchant rather than an archangel, to the counting house—'profits' . . . 'weigh' . . . 'well manag'd' . . . 'value'.

[1] *Paradise Lost*, Book VIII.

But in fact this passage is relatively calm and moderate for Milton. The core of the archangel's warning to Adam is 'take heed least Passion/sway Thy Judgement'. Milton portrayed the results of passion both in the Fall itself (the apple in *Paradise Lost* seems to act as an aphrodisiac, with a flushed and excited Eve seducing Adam) and in the ruination of Samson. Like earlier Christian writers he really saw woman as a wicked, sensual snare laid for man. If he extolled the new virtues of reason and the free will to control one's own destiny, these virtues were confined to the male sex and, moreover, appear to have been only skin-deep, always vulnerable to the machinations of womanhood. His portrayals of womanhood bear a remarkable similarity to those of Sprenger:

> *judgment scant,*
> *Capacity not rais'd to apprehend*
> *Or value what is best*
> *In choice, but oftest to affect the wrong. . . .*[1]

And like Sprenger he sees woman as a liar and a cheat, a seductive siren who cannot keep a secret once she has managed to winkle it out.

It is because man is more rational, more capable of moral rectitude than woman, that male supremacy was ordained by the Lord:

> *Therefore Gods universal Law*
> *Gave to the man despotic power*
> *Over his female in due awe,*
> *Nor from that right to part an hour,*
> *Smile she or lowre:*
> *So shall he least confusion draw*
> *On his whole life, not sway'd*
> *By female usurpation, nor dismay'd.*[2]

However, since Milton believed in the concept of free will, it followed that man had only himself to blame if he allowed passion to take control, and Samson willingly admitted that the disasters

---

[1] *Samson Agonistes.*   [2] Ibid.

which had befallen him were his own fault—and the fault, like Adam's, was giving in to the seductive wiles of the female of the species.

'It is an irrational act, and therefore not fit for a rational creature, to love any one farther than reason will allow us,' wrote Baxter in the *Christian Directory* (1678),[1] and Milton put forward the same view:

> *In loving thou dost well, in passion not,*
> *Wherein true Love consists not; love refines*
> *The thoughts, and heart enlarges, hath his seat*
> *In Reason, and is judicious, is the scale*
> *By which to heav'nly Love thou maist ascend,*
> *Not sunk in carnal pleasure, for which cause*
> *Among the Beasts no Mate for thee was found.*[2]

A very cold-blooded affair, if not downright inhuman—at best a kind of disinterested, lordly affection, totally aphysical.

The idea of a judicious, controlled affection was bound up with the notion of man as the *paterfamilias*, responsible for the economic and moral welfare of a whole household, wife, children and servants, the family being a microcosm of the state. Obviously a breadwinner gains an automatic right to dictate to his dependants on moral questions, and no doubt the Puritan patriarch, with his private line through conscience to his personal God, made ample use of his authoritarian position. He could always be relied upon to be holier than thou.

Although ultimately the dictates of organized religion come from the same source as those of the private moral conscience, the older, externalized authority of the voice of God did at least have a kind of colourful majesty. The voice from behind the mask reverberates in a terrifying fashion, and the dangerous woman is absolutely scarlet, demonic, witchlike. In comparison the split image of woman that the capitalist revolution was to produce was very tame and colourless. Before, as Sprenger put it, we had Eva and her opposite Ave, representing the two polarities, the downfall of man and his redemption, on the one hand the harlots of Jeru-

---

[1] Quoted by R. H. Tawney in *Religion and the Rise of Capitalism.*
[2] *Paradise Lost*, Book VIII.

salem, a whole host of Jezebels, and on the other only the Virgin Mary to redress the balance. Once Mammon replaced God we only had the respectable middle-class wife as opposed to the working-class prostitute, saved from a fate worse than death not by God, but by financial security and a cosy marriage—though as usual the terrible Lilith hovered threateningly on the edge of the scene, daring to publish outrageous novels, smoking cigars and gabbling on about her imaginary rights.

In a society where men have an overriding interest in the acquisition of wealth, and where women have themselves become a form of property, the link between sexuality and money becomes inextricable. Sexuality then has to be strictly controlled, not just because allowing woman to sway male passions becomes a way for woman to gain control, but because all sexual relations with women become either a way of spending money, or amount to stealing another man's property. Sexual theft may involve a man in monetary claims for compensation, thus putting money at risk, or there is a taboo on stealing because you do not want anyone to steal from you (the fundamental reason for 'respect for property' is that you want other people to respect yours). If 'honour' demands that you do not seduce the wife or daughter of another man it is because all men are 'on their honour' to leave each other's women alone, a tacit pact that can only work if everyone abides by it.

Mary Douglas[1] quotes an example of this principle carried to its most absurd limits. The Yurok of Northern California were very interested in acquiring wealth in the form of furs, shells, and feathers, and for them the quickest way of acquiring wealth was to demand compensation for adultery. As a result Yurok men came to believe that sexual contact with women would destroy their capacity for acquiring wealth, and that women and money should not be brought in contact. So sexual intercourse could not take place indoors, where a man kept his possessions, and as a result total celibacy was observed during the cold winter months—confirmed by the fact that Yurok babies tended to arrive nine months

[1] Mary Douglas, *Purity and Danger*.

after the first fine weather. Margaret Mead[1] found a similar attitude in the Manus tribe, where there was such a close tie between women and property that adultery was always a threat to the economic system. These people devalued sex, were prudish and tended to equate the sex act with the excretory functions and, perhaps most significant of all, had commercial prostitution, which is rare in primitive communities.

It sounds like a miniature version of the Victorian era, when lust was relegated to the back stairs, and found its illicit outlet in prostitutes and maidservants. In an urbanized age of extremes of wealth and poverty the respectable, wealthy *bourgeoisie* were so overtly prudish that even pianos had to have their legs concealed, but prostitution flourished on an unprecedented scale. Since working-class women were particularly badly paid a large proportion subsidized their earnings by prostitution. Virtue was a middle- and upper-class luxury which they quite simply could not afford, however many tracts and Bibles those virtuous society ladies might distribute. And although those same ladies would promptly dismiss a maidservant for having gone to bed with the young master, it was in fact a foregone conclusion that the young master would have to sow his wild oats somewhere, and the obvious place was among the servants, whose virtues would be forfeit somewhere or other before long. The prostitute, wrote Lecky in his *History of European Morals*, was

> ultimately the most efficient guardian of virtue. But for her, the unchallenged purity of countless happy homes would be polluted, and not a few who, in the pride of their untempted chastity, think of her with an indignant shudder would have known the agony of remorse and despair.[1]

Thus the working class provided a kind of sexual sewer for the wealthy. It is important to remember just how classbound the sentimental, idealized image of womanhood actually was.

One of the ways in which the sexual taboos of the time were enforced was by maintaining that respectable women had no sexual feelings, and were motivated only by wifely submission and a love

[1] Margaret Mead, *Male and Female*.
[2] W. E. H. Lecky, *History of European Morals*, Vol. ii, Chap. 5.

of motherhood. This viewpoint served a double purpose: on the one hand it justified the double standard and made it seem a positive favour on the part of the husband to take his attentions elsewhere, since sex was such a disgusting wifely duty, and absolved the husband from even trying to be a satisfactory lover; and on the other it discouraged the wife from making sexual demands or being unfaithful if her physical needs were not satisfied, since, if she ever felt or recognized such desires in herself, she would be far too ashamed to admit that she had them, even to herself. The whole notion, together with its motivation, is expressed by William Acton:

> . . . there can be no doubt that sexual feeling in the female is in the majority of cases in abeyance. . . . Many men, and particularly young men, form their ideas of women's feelings from what they notice early in life among loose or, at least, low and vulgar women . . . such women however give a very false idea of the condition of female sexual feeling in general. . . . The best mothers, wives, and managers of households, know little or nothing of sexual indulgences. Love of home, children, and domestic duties, are the only passions they feel.
>
> As a general rule, a modest woman seldom desires any sexual gratification for herself. She submits to her husband, but only to please him; and, but for the desire of maternity, would far rather be relieved from his attention. No nervous or feeble young man need, therefore, be deterred from marriage by an exaggerated notion of the duties required from him.[1]

This is one way of protecting oneself against feelings of sexual inadequacy, of slaying the image of the female who can never be satisfied. Prostitutes need not be given pleasure either, since they are paid for their services. Notice that sexual desires make one not only immodest but, by implication, a bad housekeeper, wife and mother.

Ironically, of course, given the right social conditions, this attitude can really work. When modern woman discovered the orgasm it was (combined with modern birth control) perhaps the biggest single nail in the coffin of male dominance, certainly the end of the double standard; a hundred years ago the young and virgin bride,

[1] William Acton, *The Function and Disorders of the Reproductive Organs*. A revealing study of Acton in relation to Victorian morality in general and to nineteenth-century pornography in particular is provided by Steven Marcus in *The Other Victorians*.

whose husband thought it unnecessary or impossible to give his wife pleasure, and who therefore lacked both the skill and the motivation to try to do so, was doomed to spend a lifetime with little or no understanding of her own need or capacity for physical pleasure. The prevailing attitude would also make her very inhibited, and as a result it is hardly surprising that there was so much female neurosis amongst the well-to-do. Sexual tension was unrecognized and repressed, and became tension of another sort—combine this repression with the social repression of activity confined largely to the drawing-room and one gets a pretty appalling picture. Modern research has shown that female sexual response, which is not necessary for procreation and which is apparently unknown amongst the primates, is largely a learned response. The sexual excitability of women varies enormously, but a large majority of women do not reach orgasm until they have had months or even years of sexual experience.[1] Even amongst experienced women it is rare for orgasm to be reached on each occasion, and because males have only an imperfect and inadequate knowledge of female responses the fact is that only masturbation provides woman with sexual stimulation that regularly results in orgasm. And these are the findings of research carried out on people of the twentieth century, on women who expect to reach orgasm and men who know that this expectation must be met. Whilst this expectation was missing and, even worse, female sexual desires were repressed, being either not admitted or not recognized for what they were, it is probable that many 'respectable' women were totally frigid throughout their adult lives. This is one more instance of the way in which people fit into the external norms presented by society, the way the image can become reality. The fact that it concerns such a basic urge should give us pause for thought.

This male-inspired morality did produce one ironic backlash. Sexual taboos (or a code of morality) cannot be effective unless they are accepted by society as a whole, and that means both men and women: one of the reasons that a patriarchal society has been able to work for so long is that women are themselves ready to play the roles assigned to them, never having been made aware of any

[1] Kinsey, *Sexual Behaviour in the Human Female.*

alternative. In the nineteenth century the backlash came from many sternly moral feminists, who protested against the double standard of morality, but did not claim sexual freedom for themselves—instead they wanted the male to be as virtuous and restrained as they were themselves required to be.

It is not only the prostitute who is purchased, of course. In a wealthy society, and this tends to coincide with women withdrawing from labour or being excluded from it, so that they become financial dependants, the wife is also purchased, and marriage becomes a form of legalized prostitution. Dowries may effectively offset the lack of personal charm, which itself becomes an economic asset. As long as there are economic advantages to be had for a woman through marriage, as opposed to economic disadvantages in not marrying, an element of favours purchased will remain in some cases of marriage, though not necessarily all. The elderly millionaire who marries a string of young, attractive women who are later pensioned off with a handsome alimony is only the extreme example of this principle at work—it is hypocritical to pretend that such wealthy men are made somehow unhappy or emotionally unstable by their great wealth (and the unhappy millionaire has become part of our modern mythology) and that this accounts for their promiscuity. They are only doing what other men would do if they could afford to—buying exclusive rights in a woman for as long as they want her, and then moving on. The majority of men cannot afford to pension off even one woman and must take their pleasures furtively where and how they can—an uneasy game, since they are then easily caught between conflicting demands which they cannot meet.

But there are other reasons why a well-to-do, capitalist society should encourage the image of woman staying within the confines of the home. To begin with, wives themselves become a status symbol, a form of property. In societies which are not monogamous a wealthy chief will display his status by the number of his wives, in a monogamous society a man has to confine himself to obtaining one woman and will pick one for her outstanding rank or beauty. If she has useful connections or access to money she becomes a business asset as well as a status symbol. As the latter she will show her paces by charming other men in her role as hostess, underline her husband's class and taste by impeccable behaviour, and display the potency of his wealth or earning capacity by wearing expensive clothes and jewellery and being sufficiently unoccupied to spend her time being groomed by hairdressers and manicurists. A highly elaborate and expensive dish, in fact, to be mussed up at his pleasure. Thus it is nowadays common practice, particularly in America where the traditional role of womanhood is more strongly upheld than elsewhere, to interview wives as well as husbands for higher executive jobs. For the poor man a beautiful woman may imply sexual potency, for the wealthy man it implies economic potency. And the very fact that he can afford to keep her in idleness is important—for the poor man a wife is ultimately a housekeeper who works as hard as he himself does, whose labour is necessary both inside and outside the home for the survival of the family; her hands get roughened, her figure goes, she can only afford new clothes and hairdos once in a while for special occasions, she is as tired as her husband by the end of the day. The working man cannot afford remarriage or even the incidental expenses of extra-marital affairs—Kinsey reports that extra-marital sex in middle age is almost exclusive to the prosperous middle classes, who are, on the other hand, far less promiscuous in their early years, in part because they are more inhibited by moral precepts and partly because at that stage they are more absorbed in the business of getting further education and launching out on to a career.

Furthermore, a free capitalist society is one that is largely employed in the production of consumer goods, and industry and big business need people with enough leisure to buy. The domesticated woman therefore becomes the main consumer. A hundred years ago it was the middle- and upper-class wife who had the leisure to buy all the knick-knacks that cluttered the Victorian drawing-room. Today we live in a capitalist society in which a very large proportion of the total production is devoted to consumer goods, goods which are mainly purchased by women. A man usually has aspirations to own a car, or to exchange the car he has for a more expensive one, but apart from that he spends little thought on buying goods, apart from a few clothes. It is the woman who is preoccupied with the purchase of furniture and fittings, bedding and curtains and carpets, interior decorating and saucepans, china and glass, a new refrigerator, cooker, washing machine, dishwashing machine, spin drier, perambulator, food mixer, television set, ironing board, this year's fashions and cosmetics—and probably a small second car as well. If an economy is booming enough for a significant number of families to afford these things at all, it is necessary for the woman of the household to have a good deal of leisure, not just to have the time to go out and choose all these articles, but to want them in the first place. There is nothing like boredom to make one want to buy things, as anyone with an hour to spare in the centre of town must know, and nothing like being at home all day for making one notice that the curtains look drab and the carpet is fraying. The woman who is out at work not only has preoccupations which prevent her from fussing about appearances, except perhaps her own, but she actually has no use for many of the consumer goods that our industries dream up. She does not want a sewing machine, her clothes and curtains are bought readymade; or a washing machine, spin drier or automatic iron, because most of her dirty linen is sent to a laundry. As her cooking is kept simple she is unlikely to make much use of food mixers or other culinary gadgets, and she probably does not spend enough time at home to invest in a colour television set, home movies or radios that can be heard in every room.

Many of the aids which are advertised as liberating the modern woman tend to have the opposite effect, because they simply change the nature of work instead of eliminating it. Machines have a certain novelty value, like toys for adults. It is certainly less tiring to put clothes in a washing machine, but the time saved does not really amount to much: the machine has to be watched, the clothes have to be carefully sorted first, stains removed by hand, buttons pushed and water changed, clothes taken out, aired and ironed. It would be more liberating to pack it all off to a laundry and not necessarily more expensive, since no capital investment is required. Similarly, if you really want to save time you do not make cakes with an electric mixer, you buy one in a shop. If one compares the image of the domesticated woman fostered by the women's magazines with the goods advertised by those periodicals, advertising which finances them, one realizes how useful a projected image can be commercially. A careful balance has to be struck: if you show a labour-saving gadget, follow it up with a complicated recipe on the next page; on no account hint at the notion that a woman could get herself a job, but instead foster her sense of her own usefulness, emphasize the creative aspect of her function as a housewife. So we get cake mixes where the cook simply adds an egg herself, to produce 'that lovely home-baked flavour the family love,' and knitting patterns that can be made by hand or, worse still, on knitting machines, which became a tremendous vogue when they were first introduced (difficult to know who would wear all those rapidly produced sweaters, which lacked the advantages of hand-made woollens). Automatic cookers are advertised by pictures of pretty young mothers taking their children to the park, not by professional women presetting the dinner before catching a bus to the office.

We see this economic process most clearly at work in the United States, because it is the wealthiest country and produces such a high proportion of consumer goods. As far as women and work is concerned the trend there has been decidedly retrograde in recent years. The proportion of women taking higher education has dropped considerably since the last war, and a large proportion of the girls who do go on to college are being trained for ill-paid stopgap jobs below their real ability or are taking courses not designed to equip them to work at all, but simply to make them more self-conscious in their role as wives and mothers.[1] Because American women have a great deal of leisure but have early on opted out of public affairs and business life, they tend to form powerful pressure groups to influence public affairs indirectly instead of involving themselves directly, and this method of wheeling and dealing behind the scenes can be pernicious. The average earnings of women are lower than those of negroes (if male), and the ideal American woman lives in a suburban house, having married at twenty years of age, drives her kids to and from school in the second family car, pushes labour-saving buttons and joins

[1] See Betty Friedan, *The Feminine Mystique*.

in group activities with other women like herself; self-conscious about the role of woman, child dependency and home comforts, she has a smattering of psychology, has been educated in marital relationships at college, goes to an analyst or group therapy when things go wrong, and appreciates the liberal arts. Rousseau would have approved the image. The other extreme is in Russia, where all women below middle age must work, where equal pay and opportunity are a reality, and the self-perpetuating cycle of consumer goods hardly exists. If the end-result is not very attractive to Western women it is simply because life in Russia is harsh for everyone, men and women. Somewhere between must lie a happy medium, with freedom of choice on the kind of life you want to lead, with work done because it is absorbing and satisfying, not because long hours of drudgery are necessary for survival, nor because consumer goods provide a compulsion which cannot be resisted.

IV

Rousseau, Revolution, Romanticism
and Retrogression

Once God as a reality was dead and the pleasures of an expanding Mammon could be enjoyed by the new *bourgeoisie* with only a modicum of moral restraint, a reaction was bound to come, for patriarchal and other reasons, and come it did. Everyone who could afford it had flocked into the towns to enjoy a world of opera, theatre, social visiting and card-playing, and life in the country was considered dreadfully dull. In England the literature of the period following the Restoration is full of criticism of the behaviour of the leisured classes, and particularly of women. John Evelyn looked back with regret at the womanhood of earlier days, and one recognizes the Puritan image:

> Men courted and chose their wives for their modesty, frugality, keeping at home, good housewifery, and other economical virtues then in reputation, and the young damsels were taught all these in the country in their parent's houses. . . . The virgins and young ladies of that golden age put their hands to the spindle, nor disdained they the needle; were helpful to their parents, instructed in the management of a family, and gave promise of making excellent wives.

But once wealth increases frugality and the domestic virtues are no longer so much in demand. Instead of spinning and sewing women were ordering extravagant clothes from dressmakers and enjoying the social advantages of town life, one of which was certainly shopping.

The vapid lives of society women became an increasingly popular target for writers, and although education for girls was limited to those arts necessary to charm a potential husband, like music and dancing, the eighteenth-century men of letters were by and large in favour of women getting a broader education. Dr. Johnson approved of educated women and said that men who did not were frightened of being outstripped by their womenfolk; Richardson, Daniel Defoe and Addison pleaded for a more comprehensive education for women. Since women were the hostesses in the urban drawing-rooms it is natural that intellectual men should have been attracted to those women whose conversation was not limited to trivia, to drawing-rooms where interesting conversation was more important than endless card-playing. The famous salons of Paris in the seventeenth and eighteenth centuries with their brilliant hostesses found a more modest counterpart in London. Mrs. Montagu ran a salon which gave birth to the phrase 'bluestocking'. The blue stockings, originally worn by men, were probably an imitation of the *bas bleu* assemblies of Paris, at the salon of Madame de Polignac in the Rue St. Honoré, where the wearing of blue stockings was all the rage.

Samuel Pepys found that going out to enjoy the amusements of London on his own made his uneducated wife thoroughly miserable—and thus difficult to live with. He began giving her lessons in arithmetic and geography almost as a form of therapy. He also encouraged her to take singing and dancing lessons, and finally relented from his habitual meanness to give her a fairly generous dress allowance. The 'spleen' became a fashionable disorder for women with not enough to do, and the cure was to remove oneself to the social delights of a watering town, where the round of pleasure began once more. By the eighteenth century writers like Swift and Pope were vigorously satirizing the empty-headedness of ladies of leisure, who spent one half of their lives at their toilet and the other at the card table, 'Never to hold her tongue a minute;/ While all she prates has nothing in't.' The friendships—as opposed to amorous relationships—between men of letters and intelligent, educated women is a feature of the period. Mrs. Thrale regularly played hostess to Dr. Johnson, and Fanny Burney was sometimes amongst the guests. Lady Mary Wortley Montagu corresponded with Pope.

But these people were of course a small *élite*, whilst the majority of the well-to-do pursued more frivolous pleasures. The reaction when it came attacked both the social inequality on which this life of pleasure was based, and the values implicit in this urban way of life, and the prime instigator was Jean Jacques Rousseau. At the same time, and this is the most important aspect of his thought for our present purpose, he put woman firmly back in the home. The pleasures of civilized life might be unhealthy for the whole of mankind, but they were particularly bad for woman. It was important for mankind's moral welfare that he should get back to a more natural way of life. Man, he thought, was 'naturally' and fundamentally good, it was the artificial state of society that corrupted him, and so it was necessary to strip everything away and get back to a state of nature. Woman's role as a mother was at once very important and very limited in Rousseau's vision: as a wife and mother she exerted an important moral influence, but here her role began and ended.

Nowadays it is difficult for us to understand the enormous influence that Rousseau had on his own and succeeding generations. His *Social Contract* was the Bible of the French Revolution, illogical as the book now seems to us it was as influential in France then as *Das Kapital* later became in Russia; Robespierre was his devout disciple, and his remains were given reburial in the Pantheon. 'The spirit which animated the Revolution was the spirit of Rousseau. From the Declaration of the Rights of Man to the formation of the Constitution in 1793, there is no important act in which the influence of the Genevese philosopher is not discernible,' wrote G. H. Lewes in his biography of Robespierre. But his influence was not confined to the political radicals of his day. The whole gamut of reactions and attitudes which we now cover with the umbrella term 'the Romantic Revolution' is directly attributable to Rousseau. The emphasis on subjective emotion, on sensibility, the glorification of natural landscape as a manifestation of a vague, thoroughly subjective pantheism are largely due to the influence of Rousseau. Of course the interraction between significant men and the times they live in can be a subject for endless debate, but in the case of Rousseau I think it is fair to say that he was more

Rousseau, Revolution, Romanticism and Retrogression

the father of his times than the child of his times. Certainly he had an enormous influence on the intellectual life of the eighteenth and nineteenth centuries. Apart from political thought his ideas were germinal both for idealist philosophy and for literature: Wordsworth seems like an extension of the spirit of Rousseau, George Eliot when she was merely a young woman called Mary Ann Evans shocked Emerson by declaring that the *Confessions* was her favourite book, Tolstoy read and re-read Rousseau and the Tolstoyism of his later years is largely an extension of the Genevese philosopher's ideas, whilst his patriarchal attitudes on woman's role being confined to motherhood are similar to Rousseau's. As far as women are concerned, the image projected by the early romantic poets and later sentimentalized so appallingly by the mid-nineteenth century has its origins in Rousseau. Wordsworth's poem 'She was a phantom of delight' expresses the original romantic image:

> *She was a Phantom of delight*
> *When first she gleamed upon my sight;*
> *A lovely Apparition, sent*
> *To be a moment's ornament;*
> *Her eyes as stars of Twilight fair;*
> *Like Twilight's, too, her dusky hair;*
> *But all things else about her drawn*
> *From May-time and the cheerful Dawn;*
> *A dancing Shape, an Image gay,*
> *To haunt, to startle, and way-lay.*

But once the musing male has been way-laid by her female charms, we get down to the heart of the matter. Her real purpose, romantically idealized, of course, is to be a helpmate to man, devoted to domesticity:

> *I saw her upon nearer view,*
> *A Spirit, yet a Woman too!*
> *Her household motions light and free,*
> *And steps of virgin-liberty;*
> *A countenance in which did meet*

Rousseau, Revolution, Romanticism and Retrogression

Sweet records, promises as sweet;
A creature not too bright or good
For human nature's daily food;
For transient sorrows, simple wiles,
Praise, blame, love, kisses, tears, and smiles.

This is the core of the Rousseau ideal of womanhood, who, in spite of all her sexual charms, must be essentially homespun, because once the initial business of charming and falling in love is over her duties are exclusively domestic.

Rousseau idealized the married state, which he saw as the basic unit of a natural, primeval way of life before a more complex, corrupt society had depraved human morality. Eighteenth-century society might flock to the towns to avoid the tedium of country life, but frivolous amusements are not for Julie, the ideal wife of *La Nouvelle Heloise*: 'Every evening Julie, content with her day, desires nothing different for the morrow; and every morning she beseeches Heaven for a day like the last: she does always the same things because they are good, and because she knows nothing better to do.' Rousseau always asserted that men and women's interests (though the latter were very limited) should be kept separate, and sharply differentiated sex roles were part of his idealized primeval state, where man went out to win food for the family whilst the woman minded the hut. 'Nature does not prescribe a housekeeping, sedentary life to man, as their restlessness under it amply shows,' he wrote in his *Letter to D'Alembert*. Although he gave away his own children to be brought up in a foundling hospital he gave a lot of thought to the education of children, which he regarded as the prime function of the marital unit, and it was because he emphasized woman's role as a mother that he insisted on her moral virtue, her confinement to the bounds of home. He not only made it fashionable to live in the country once more, but to breast-feed one's own child instead of hiring a wet nurse. 'See that the mothers deign to nourish their own babies, and morals will be reformed of themselves, and the sentiments of nature will be awakened in all hearts. . . . The appeal of the domestic life is the best counter-poison to bad morals. . . . When the family is

96

lively and animated, the domestic cares are the dearest occupation of the wife and the most delightful entertainment of the husband,' he wrote in Book 5 of *Emile*, which contains his most explicit views on the role and education of women. Note that domestic life is still somehow only 'entertainment' for men, a pleasurable diversion and not a central preoccupation.

The image that Rousseau fosters would not have been a bad one, had it not been based on fundamental inequality, and this is particularly ironic when one considers that Rousseau also preached a radical egalitarianism. 'Liberty, equality, fraternity' was to be applicable only to men, both in thought and deed, as we shall see later. In *Emile* Rousseau is quite explicit on the position of woman: she is to be brought up as man's subordinate, to minister to his needs and to give him pleasure. He has a good deal of sympathy for the men who 'would restrict a woman to the labours of her sex and would leave her in profound ignorance of everything else' but he sees objections to this: in the first place it would make her a prey to immoral men, secondly it would make her unfit for the duties of motherhood, and thirdly it would make her tedious company for the husband:

> A man who thinks should not ally himself with a woman who does not think, for he loses the chief delight of social life if he has a wife who cannot share his thoughts.

But a female ignoramus is infinitely preferable to the bluestocking of sophisticated Parisian society:

> But I would a thousand times rather have a homely girl, simply brought up, than a learned lady and a wit who would make a literary circle of my house and instal herself as its president. A female wit is a scourge to her husband, her children, her friends, her servants, to everybody. From the lofty heights of her genius she scorns every womanly duty, and she is always trying to make a man of herself after the fashion of Mlle. de L'Enclos. Outside her home she always makes herself ridiculous and she is very rightly a butt for criticism, as we always are when we try to escape from our own position into one for which we are unfitted. These highly talented women only get a hold over fools. We can always tell what artist or friend holds the pen or pencil when they are at work; we know what discreet man of letters dictates their oracles in private. This trickery is unworthy of

a decent woman. If she really had talents, her pretentiousness would degrade them. Her honour is to be unknown; her glory is the respect of her husband; her joys the happiness of her family.

We know that talented *salonnières* and women of letters were very far from getting a hold only on fools: they became a focal point for cultural exchange and later for radical political debate prior to and during the French Revolution. But we see here the beginning of the trend that made 'bluestocking' a pejorative word, and the familiar masculine sneer that such women were only trying to 'ape' men.

The idea that woman could achieve nothing requiring mental powers (here implied by the suggestion that the intellectual products of women had really been produced by their male lovers) was also one that was to gain ground, one could almost say in proportion to the amount actually achieved by women. The fundamental distinction between male and female roles, to be given reality by a fundamental distinction in male and female education was, throughout the nineteenth century, justified on the grounds that woman's intellect was inferior anyway, or at least of a different nature, and Rousseau, having demanded the almost total exclusion of women from intellectual activity and wider education, also discovered the justification:

> The search for abstract and speculative truths, for principles and axioms in science, for all that tends to wide generalisation, is beyond a woman's grasp; their studies should be thoroughly practical. It is their business to apply the principles discovered by men, it is their place to make the observations which lead men to discover those principles. A woman's thoughts, beyond the range of her immediate duties, should be directed to the study of men, or the acquirement of that agreeable learning whose sole end is the formation of taste; for the works of genius are beyond her reach, and she has neither the accuracy nor the attention for success in the exact sciences. . . .

This kind of thing was repeated with variations throughout the nineteenth century *ad nauseam*, and the attitude is still not dead today. Some men say baldly that women's intellects are inferior to those of men, and that women are incapable of genius. Rousseau himself said that no woman ever had 'the heavenly fire of genius' in his *Letter to D'Alembert*; other men politely veil their conviction of female inferiority by saying that the female mind is 'different', but they almost always mean 'inferior', which is obvious when one studies the differences they list: woman is intuitive rather than rational, she is better at applied science than abstract thought. Not only does this distinction give men a sense of innate superiority, it also justifies subordination. Even when woman is given education and admitted gradually into the professions and employment, she is always one rung lower down the ladder: the secretary, not the manager; the nurse, not the doctor, laboratory assistant, not research scientist. Of course the real reason is that the manager, the doctor and the research scientist are better paid than the nurse, secretary and laboratory assistant. In fact the latter jobs would not have been and have not been done by women until not enough men were interested in doing such menial and ill-paid jobs. A hundred years ago the personal secretary was invariably male.

As far as Rousseau himself was concerned his attitude on women, his conviction that they should be trained for the pleasure of man, is particularly ironic and illogical in view of his egalitarian political principles. 'Man is born free, and everywhere he is in chains' thunders the inspiring if philosophically unsound first line of the *Social Contract*, and if one had not read any of his other works one might remain under the blissful illusion that when he uses the word 'man' he means 'mankind'. In fact one might suspect that Rousseau deliberately fosters the illusion: throughout the book he never mentions the word 'woman' at all, and one gets the impression of a unisexual universe. Speaking of the family as the first form of human society he refers only to the authority of the father, and the children's attachment to him, without any reference to motherhood at all, even though the function of motherhood was, in other works, given as his main justification for the confinement of woman to the home and the sexual double standard.

Because Rousseau carefully avoids the topic of female subordination in the *Social Contract*, because his attitude would have made utter nonsense of his view that government should always strive to redress the balance of equality, iron out inequalities, of his whole concept of government as an expression of the popular will, one can say that the women of revolutionary France were thoroughly conned, and once the Revolution was firmly established this proved to be the case.

Women played a very significant role in the French Revolution, and at all levels. In the years before and after the storming of the Bastille the salons of Paris became the debating ground for political radicals of various factions. The Girondist party was born in the salon of Mme. Roland, the republicans met at the home of Mme. Robert, and the drawing-room of Mme. de Genlis became a focal point for the Orleanist party. Women also played an active part in the political clubs that sprouted up like mushrooms, and several women were acclaimed for their rousing political oratory. When Mlle. Théroigne, who was one of the heroines of the famous insurrection of women at Versailles, and who later ran a salon, addressed the Jacobin club in 1792 she aroused great feminist fervour in her male admirers. 'If our fathers', said one enthusiast, 'had so poor an opinion of women, it was because they were not free.' Théroigne also achieved a great oratorical success at the famous Cordeliers club, where women played a prominent part. And at street level, so to speak, we know how enthusiastic the female revolutionaries were: it was the deputation of women that invaded the Assembly at Versailles and brought the King back to Paris. '*Les femmes furent a l'avant garde de notre Révolution—Il ne faut pas s'en étonner, elles souffraient d'avantage,*' wrote Michelet. But once the groundwork was done the position of women changed: in 1793 the National Convention suppressed all women's clubs and societies, closed the salons, and denied women all political rights. This was in fact not only a betrayal but represented a position even worse than before the Revolution, since during the *ancien régime* women with certain property qualifications had been able to vote and occasionally even sat in provincial assemblies. Later Napoleon, who despised women and considered them utterly irresponsible, reinforced male domination: the Code Napoleon decreed that a woman should obey her husband, that a father had sole authority over his children, and that a woman could not go to law without her husband's consent.

One cannot help feeling that if those French women had been

able to compare the *Social Contract* with *Emile* the course of history might have been very different. 'To renounce one's liberty is to renounce one's quality as a man, the rights and also the duties of humanity'—but in fact liberty, or perhaps humanity itself is an all-male affair, since he writes of women in *Emile*: 'They must be trained to bear the yoke from the first, so that they may not feel it, to master their own caprices and to submit themselves to the will of others.' This accords somewhat ill with his diatribes against despotism, and his almost mathematical allocation of freedom as part of a popular will. Apparently woman has no part in the social contract at all, no freedom, no rights. Nor does Rousseau have any illusions about the nature of subordination, he may ramble on in his other works about woman being naturally modest and retiring, formed by nature to submit to man, but in the *Social Contract* he takes issue with Aristotle and denies that there is any such thing as a 'natural' slave:

> Slaves lose everything in their bonds, even the desire to escape from them; they love their servitude as the companions of Ulysses loved their brutishness. If then, there are slaves by nature, it is because there have been slaves contrary to nature. The first slaves were made such by force; their cowardice kept them in bondage.

So, one is forced to conclude, man is born free, but woman should definitely be kept in chains. Perhaps, to absolve Rousseau from the charge of blatant hypocrisy in the *Social Contract*, one should take it as read that whereas men have been made unequal by society, women are basically weaker and therefore more subordinate, a state of nature due to physical difference and not social development? But this will not wash, since Rousseau concludes the first book of the *Social Contract* 'with a remark which ought to serve as a basis for the whole social system; it is that instead of destroying natural equality, the fundamental pact, on the contrary, substitutes a moral and lawful equality for the physical inequality which nature imposed upon men, so that, although unequal in strength or intellect, they all become equal by convention and legal right'. He is similarly two-faced on the subject of economics: in *Emile* he justifies the subordination of woman by saying that she might as well make the best of it anyhow, since she has no alternative and 'is dependent on our feelings, on the price we put upon her virtue, and the opinion we have of her charms and her deserts'; whereas in the *Social Contract* he says 'as to wealth, no citizen should be rich enough to be able to buy another, and none poor enough to be forced to sell himself'. And yet the perpetuation and reinforcement of sexual role-playing which he favoured, both within marriage and outside it, depended on just this principle.

It is a curious fact, and perhaps indicative of the overwhelming influence of Rousseau, the awe and veneration with which he was regarded, that Mary Wollstonecraft should have written her *Vindication of the Rights of Woman* as an answer to Rousseau's views on woman's education, or rather, non-education, without once pointing out that his attitude made nonsense of his egalitarian ideals. I must admit that I found this extremely perplexing at first. I think the answer must lie in her own passionate political beliefs, after all, she married William Godwin. Her own book on the French Revolution, which she witnessed at first hand, reveals that she was as much a passionate disciple of Rousseau as the French revolutionaries: 'The will of the people being supreme, it is not only the duty of their representatives to respect it, but their political existence ought to depend on their acting conformably to the will of their constituents.' Not only was she a disciple of Rousseau on a political level, she was a creature of his type of romantic sensibility and subjective pantheism. After her death Godwin wrote a tribute to his wife, entitled *Memoirs of Mary Wollstonecraft*, in which he said: 'She found an inexpressible delight in the beauties of nature, and in the splendid reveries of the imagination. But nature itself, she thought, would be no better than a vast blank, if the mind of the observer did not supply it with an animating soul.' Mary Wollstonecraft was prepared to take issue against Rousseau, the god of her own and succeeding generations, when it came to the position of her own sex, but she could only do it half-heartedly because to make a thorough job of it would have meant destroying the world she believed in, discovering that the god had feet of clay.

For Rousseau the natural man belonged to a golden age uncorrupted by human society. He was a gentle, rather solitary creature who wandered through the primeval forest, harming no one, occasionally satisfying his sexual appetite on some female encountered on the way. The beginnings of social life, and for Rousseau the ideal stage of human development, was when man and woman moved into a hut together, and conjugal and paternal love were born. 'Each family became a small society, that much more united because reciprocal affection and liberty were the only ties; and it was then that the first difference in the way in which the two sexes lived, which up to that time had been the same, was established. The women became more sedentary, and became accustomed to looking after the hut and the children, whilst the man went out to seek their common subsistence.' This idyllic but obviously fallacious picture of the noble savage at home comes from the *Discours sur L'Origine de L'Inégalité parmi les Hommes*, which gives us the most comprehensive picture of Rousseau's idea of primitive life and also gives us some clue to the logic behind the romantic image of woman, the way in which she could be at once idealized and subordinated, regarded as intellectually inferior but morally superior—very much the standard attitude during the nineteenth century.

For Rousseau aggression was not a basic and inherent characteristic of man but one imposed upon him by a developing society. The noble savage, according to the *Discours sur L'Origine de L'Inégalité* is so tender-hearted that he would not willingly hurt a fly, and the prime virtue which Rousseau accords him is pity, which modern sociologists and anthropologists would find very curious. Pity, says Rousseau, was the result of man's awareness of his own vulnerability, and arose from weakness, not strength. Elaborating on the attribute of pity, 'a suitable characteristic for creatures as weak and subject to as many evils as we are', he immediately goes on to find this characteristic very evident in creatures even weaker —animals and women. Women are mothers, and he praises 'the tenderness of mothers for their little ones, and the dangers which they brave on their behalf'. Moreover, this virtue is not only associated with weakness, but it is put in direct opposition to the rational faculty. Pity, says Rousseau, depends on the ability to identify with another suffering creature, 'and it is obvious that this identification must have been much closer in the state of nature than in a rational state of mind. It is reason which gives birth to self-esteem, and it is reflection which strengthens it. . . . It is philosophy which isolates a man; it is through philosophy that a man will secretly say, on seeing a man suffer: Die, if you will, I am safe'.

I think most people would today agree that pity and the ability to feel for others depends on strength rather than weakness, is a fairly cultivated emotion which implies a degree of civilization. But if we turn back the clock and remember the enormous influence of Rousseau's ideas during the latter half of the eighteenth century and the first half of the nineteenth, one can begin to see how it was possible to regard woman as both inferior and superior. Woman was constantly referred to as being rather childlike (which was supposed to make her naturally suitable for the care of children), and her natural sympathy and tender heart were emphasized. On the other hand she was incapable of rational thought, and the very strength of her feelings interfered with any rational faculty she might possess. Woman, it was said over and over again, was nearer to the primitive state of man. 'It has long been observed', wrote James McGrigor Allan in a book entitled *Woman Suffrage Wrong* published in 1890, 'that among people progressing in civilisation, men are in advance of women' and the observation had indeed been made throughout the century, as Havelock Ellis was to admit with shame for his sex. By that time the noble savage had been lost sight of and the argument was simply another weapon to prove woman generally inferior. The same Mr. Allan is of course still eulogizing on woman's function as a wife and mother, not because he really respects her in those functions, but because he wants to divert her from demanding the vote: 'In all languages, the words *Wife, Mother* are spoken with reverence, and associated with the highest, holiest functions of woman's earthly life. To man belongs the kingdom of the head: to woman the empire of the heart! . . . In every pure and legitimate relation—as daughter, sister, wife, mother—woman is the direct assistant of individual man. . . . Not woman's enlightened advisers and true friends, are those who encourage her to risk all that solid power, and legitimate sovereignty which she now exerts over man, (swaying him by her beauty, good temper, good sense, womanly graces, accomplishments, and instinctive tact) to try a wild experiment, and rush into a revolt which can only end in ignominious and ridiculous defeat.' More than a century earlier Rousseau had written in *Emile*:

> Woman's reign is a reign of gentleness, tact, and kindness; her commands are caresses, her threats are tears. She should reign in the home as a minister reigns in the state, by contriving to be ordered to do what she wants.

The fact that—had he been writing in the *Social Contract*—Rousseau would immediately have advocated the overthrow of such a state is conveniently forgotten! And just as Mr. Allan says the woman's function in life is to be 'the direct assistant of individual man; supporter, consoler, renovator, preserver of the human race; or, as comprehensively summed up in Holy Writ, man's *help-meet*' Rousseau had advised that woman's education should be planned in relation to man:

> To be pleasing in his sight, to win his respect and love, to train him in childhood, to tend him in manhood, to counsel and console, to make his life pleasant and happy, these are the duties of woman for all time, and this is what she should be taught while she is young.

Of course woman was being, and continued to be educated in relation to man's requirements, and (as we saw in our first chapter) an official government adviser on education can still advocate the same line in the middle of the twentieth century. The result has been a form of narcissism and a degree of psychological dependence on social approval which is regarded as part of the female character by modern psychologists. 'A man says what he knows,' wrote Rousseau in *Emile*, 'a woman says what will please':

> You should not check a girl's prattle like a boy's by the harsh question, 'What is the use of that?' but by another question at least as difficult to answer, 'What effect will that have?'

The very fact that the subtitle of *Emile* is *On Education* reveals that Rousseau's so-called natural woman was made and not born. She is still being made. 'Numerous studies have shown that girls are more conforming, more suggestible, and more dependent upon the opinion of others than boys,' wrote Eleanor Maccoby[1] in a book published in this decade. This personality trait, so intimately connected with the patterns of courtship in our society, where the male must still make the advances and the female's sense of belonging and self-respect depends on the approval accorded her by the males of the society, does not, among other things, make for intellectual originality.

Rousseau's attitude to the relationship between the sexes not only fostered narcissism, it actually encouraged masochism as well, and this is also a female personality trait discussed at length by psychologists. Naturally masochism tends to be associated with passivity. Rousseau and almost everyone since associated femininity with passivity, though of course in the male mind female passivity has distinct advantages—he wants to make the advances and he is able to, because the man who pays the piper calls the tune. Rousseau shuddered at the very notion of women making sexual advances, which he regarded as 'immodest', and female modesty was greatly emphasized throughout the nineteenth century. It would, for example, have been highly immodest for a woman to enter the hurlyburly of active politics, as Mr. Allan, amongst many others, was quick to point out: 'Physical courage is exclusively a male virtue. Women are constitutionally timid, and their chief virtue is modesty. Any great and unusual exhibition of bravery by a woman, or violent excitement, especially the loud, intemperate language of quarrel, with vehement gestures, or manual conflict, almost always causes hysterical reaction, most injurious to health, dangerous, and sometimes fatal: conclusive testimony that woman was never intended to rival man, either in politics or war. The senate, bar, platform, barrack, guardroom and battle-field do not foster womanly virtues.'

But passivity and modesty are not enough, submission is called for, and this has a distinctly masochistic flavour. Rousseau, having advised that women should be 'trained to bear the yoke from the first, so that they may not feel it', goes on to say that woman should above all be gentle and docile, since

---

[1] *The Development of Sex Differences*, edited by Eleanor E. Maccoby, p. 43.

formed to obey a creature as imperfect as man, a creature often vicious and always faulty, she should learn to submit to injustice and to suffer the wrongs inflicted on her by her husband without complaint; she must be gentle for her own sake, not his. Bitterness and obstinacy only multiply the sufferings of the wife and the misdeeds of the husband. . . .

Fine words from the father of the French Revolution! The passage makes one recall St. Augustine's description of his virtuous mother. *Plus ça change.* . . .

Coventry Patmore's lengthy poem *The Angel in the House* was very popular and represented the Victorian ideal of marriage and womanhood, and here the submission to male authority has taken a decidedly kinky turn. The woman does not submit and accept humiliation as a form of passive resistance and self-preservation, she positively enjoys the experience, it becomes 'exhilirating' and a 'rapture', or at least the male author preferred to think so:

> *Her soul, that once with pleasure shook,*
> *Did any eyes her beauty own,*
> *Now wonders how they dare to look*
> *On what belongs to him alone;*
> *The indignity of taking gifts*
> *Exhilirates her loving breast;*
> *A rapture of submission lifts*
> *Her life into celestial rest;*
> *There's nothing left of what she was;*
> *Back to the babe the woman dies,*
> *And all the wisdom that she has*
> *Is to love him for being wise.*

Note that the narcissism which, as Mary Wollstonecraft pointed out, will not stop after marriage if a woman is educated to please, has here been firmly killed off in the married woman, to ensure that the girl who was a charming coquette, educated to lure men on and titillate their desires, should not misbehave after marriage. Tolstoy took the same attitude to the married woman, being a very jealous man himself, which was why he made Natasha such a dumpily unattractive matron after her marriage, and why he was so vituperative about women being kept unnaturally attractive through artificial birth control in *The Kreutzer Sonata*, where a man murders his wife for a suspected infidelity. The poor woman, not being constantly pregnant, had become a danger to the marriage, maddening her husband with unfounded suspicions. However, to do Tolstoy justice he does not imply that the wife would actually enjoy or invite a murderous assault.

It is interesting to consider the world as it now is, and speculate just how far Rousseau is responsible for the relatively backward position of women in the Western world today. When one remembers that the revolution which came so much later to Russia was based, not on the writings of Jean Jacques but on those of Marx and Engels, and that the latter emphasized the importance of liberating women from the tyranny of the individual domestic unit, whilst Rousseau had idealized the domestic unit (and nineteenth-century German philosophers who discussed marriage and justified the subordinate position of women still praised marriage as a microcosm of the state) one wonders just how far individual philosophers have influenced the very different roles played by women in the West as opposed to Russia and other Communist countries in the world today. Of course the time element has something to do with it, which is also why the first women prime ministers have come to the fore in new states, but more important is the fact that the Russian Revolution was so much more radical, whilst in the West the capitalist system went on flourishing, with only minor modifications. The German philosophers who, as we shall see, went on justifying the subordination of woman, were greatly influenced by Rousseau as the prophet of freedom based on subjective will. But individual influences apart, the truth of the matter is that both Rousseau and the men who came later were not inspired by the philosophic search for truth or justice on this particular topic: the basic motive was a wish to defend an entrenched position, the wealth and power that history and the capitalist system had given to their own sex at the expense of the other. They were as eager to justify superior status and domination as other men were to prove the white man innately superior to the negro, and the romantic image of woman was a sop to the conscience, rather like the negro image of happy coal-black mammies serving in white households and cotton-picking slaves who are never so happy as when singing spirituals. When the chips are down these cosy images soon fade and we find out what the whole thing is really about. The anti-feminists then drop the flattery and become frankly abusive. 'One would wish' wrote a certain Sir Amroth Edward Wright in a slim volume entitled *The Unexpurgated Case Against Woman Suffrage* which was published, appropriately enough, in 1913, when the situation for the British male was getting somewhat desperate

> for every girl who is growing up to womanhood that it might be brought home to her by some refined and ethically-minded member of her own sex how insufferable a person woman becomes when, like a spoilt child, she exploits the indulgence of man; when she proclaims that it is his duty to serve her and to share with her his power and possessions; when she makes an outcry when he refuses to part with what is his own; and when she insists upon thrusting her society upon men everywhere.

This gentleman complained that modern education was to blame for the demand for female suffrage, woman was 'not taught the defects and limitations of the female mind' and he declared that 'the failure to recognise that man is the master, and why he is the master, lies at the root of the suffrage problem'. Man was master for three reasons: firstly he had 'superior physical force, the power of compulsion upon which all government is based', secondly he was intellectually superior, and thirdly he had 'superior money-earning capacity'. He does admit that a shortage of husbands on the one hand and starvation wages for women on the other might make woman's position rather difficult, but he declared that 'revolt is not morally justified' when there is an escape route, which in true racist fashion turns out to be emigration. Of course many women did emigrate to the far-flung Empire, if not to find work, at least husbands, but the tone of 'if you don't like it, clear out' is even more untenable than wishing to ship all coloured people back to their country of origin or Hitler's plan to send all Jews to Madagascar. After all, English women were indigenous, but apparently not only the land and the wealth and possessions belonged to the male sex alone, but woman herself was only a male possession, and as such should consider herself fortunate. Educators, according to Sir Amroth, had failed to make girls sufficiently aware of

> the great outstanding fact of the world: the fact that, turn where you will, you find individual man showering upon individual woman—one man in tribute to her enchantment, another out of a sense of gratitude, and another just because she is something that is his—every good thing which, suffrage or no suffrage, she could never have procured for herself.

However, a year after this book was published, and in spite of their superior attributes of mind, men everywhere were busy blowing their power, possessions and themselves to smithereens, and they found they could not quite manage on their own, either to keep the guns fed, to nurse the wounded or fill the jobs left undone by the dead. Luckily for Sir Amroth and the many men who thought as he did, not all women had taken his advice and set sail for Australia or the New World.

V

Mind over Matter

The further we move into the realm of modern ideas, the more we discover that patriarchal attitudes can survive intellectual change; the attitudes are transmuted, adapted, but remain fundamentally what they had been for generations. It goes to show, not just that even highly able and original minds will continue to justify a state of affairs which is advantageous, but that we are all shaped by our early memories. The family structure of childhood, with its image of father and mother, is accepted as fundamental and repeated by the child become father. And although *bourgeois* marriage may look like a trap rather than an ideal to us, this ideal of family life was reinforced in the past not only by moral constraint but, ironically, by the fact that it was so difficult to attain. Young men who wanted to reach some standing in the world had to postpone marriage until such time as they could afford it, since the wife earned nothing. Freud spent five years apart from Martha Bernays before he dared to risk marriage. 'These difficult times will not discourage me,' he wrote to her, 'so long as we remain healthy and are spared exceptional misfortune. Then we are certain to achieve what we are striving for—a little home into which sorrow may find its way, but never privation, a being-together throughout all the vicissitudes of life, a quiet contentment that will prevent us from ever having to ask what is the point of living. I know after all how sweet you are, how you can turn a house into a paradise, how you will share my interests, how gay and painstaking you will be. I will let you rule the house as much as you wish, and you will reward me with your sweet love and by rising above all those weaknesses for which women are so often despised.'[1] This

[1] *Letters of Sigmund Freud*, edited by Ernst L. Freud, p. 85.

is the nineteenth-century idyll of married life. Being an intellectual, Freud also promises to 'initiate you into things which could not interest a girl so long as she is unfamiliar with her future companion and his occupation'. But the idyll was too costly for young professional men with ambition but no private means, its attainment meant years of hard work and sexual self-restraint. Lydgate in *Middlemarch* is an awful warning of the disasters of marriage without financial security. Middle-class men married rather late in life, on average, and used working-class girls if sexual restraint became too much for them. Lecky regarded the prostitute as an unfortunate but necessary sewer, he upheld monogamy, the lifelong union of one man with one woman, as the ideal norm, but realized that, the economics of respectability being what they were, working hard was not always an effective cure against libidinous desires when early marriage was not possible. 'There are always multitudes who, in the period of their lives when their passions are most strong, are incapable of supporting children in their own social rank, and who would therefore injure society by marrying into it, but are nevertheless perfectly capable of securing an honourable career for their illegitimate children in the lower social sphere to which these would naturally belong.'[1] Tolstoy had an illegitimate son who was employed like any other serf on his estate; in *The Mill on the Floss* George Eliot describes Philip Wakem's father as having illegitimate sons for whom he provided 'in a grade of life duly beneath his own'. Once again we see just how class-bound the ideal of marriage and family life was. Thus a man's image of himself was not only bound up with his position as a paterfamilias, but his position as head of a respectable family merged with his image of himself as a respectable and respected member of society. 'The family is the centre and the archetype of the State,' wrote Lecky, 'and the happiness and goodness of society are always in a very great degree dependent upon the purity of domestic life.'

Thinking man orders his universe, builds a pyramid with himself placed automatically at the tip. All other living creatures are placed in a descending downward slope beneath him. For the philosopher man is a form of absolute, and woman must therefore be something

---

[1] W. E. H. Lecky, *History of European Morals*, Vol. II, Chapt. 5.

less. For the psychologist the 'norms' of human behaviour are identified with male behaviour, so that women are in some sense always peculiarly abnormal. The poor creature cannot help it, sighed the medieval schoolmen, she has no soul; you must make allowances, argued the men of reason, she was born without a rational faculty; how awful to be so deprived, said the analysts, sex is the fundamental urge and she was born without the wherewithal, no wonder she spends her days trying to mimic us.

If Darwin upset man's sense of his own dignity and importance it was not for long. Soon he had constructed a new pyramid, with himself at the top and apes, mammals, and other vertebrates down below. The indignity of man's animal ancestry was more than offset by the fact that he had since 'got to the top', and the idea of the survival of the fittest allowed man to extemporize on the qualities of reason, initiative, social adaptability and good physiology which had allowed him to reach his present lofty heights of civilized life. The theory of the origin of the species was not one which promoted egalitarian ideals. It not only made Rousseau's noble savage a sentimental image for dreamers and children, it was an active encouragement to self-congratulation, ambition and aggression. In an age of imperialism it encouraged the white European to regard himself as the superior of the backward races, Africans or Red Indians; in an age of class exploitation it encouraged the middle-class business man to regard himself as more capable than the working man he exploited; in an age of growing nationalism it could even appear to encourage war. A not altogether successful attempt was made to use evolutionary theory to justify male domination over women, and to prove men be naturally superior.

The first culprit was Charles Darwin himself. *The Descent of Man, and Selection in Relation to Sex* bristles with fairly obvious contradictions. He starts with an *a priori* acceptance of the usual distinction between male and female characteristics, which is really identical with the views held by Rousseau:

> Woman seems to differ from man in mental disposition, chiefly in her greater tenderness and less selfishness. . . . Woman, owing to her maternal instincts, displays these qualities towards her infants in an eminent degree; therefore it is likely that she should often extend

them towards her fellow-creatures. Man is the rival of other men; he delights in competition, and this leads to ambition which passes too easily into selfishness. These latter qualities seem to be his natural and unfortunate birthright. It is generally admitted that with woman the powers of intuition, of rapid perception, and perhaps of imitation, are more strongly marked than in man; but some, at least, of these faculties are characteristic of the lower races, and therefore of a past and lower state of civilisation.

The chief distinction in the intellectual powers of the two sexes is shewn by man attaining to a higher eminence, in whatever he takes up, than woman can attain—whether requiring deep thought, reason, or imagination, or merely the use of the senses and hands.

What is noticeable about this passage is not merely the un-questioning acceptance of the generally held views on sexual characteristics, surprising in such a scientist, but the similarity of the moral standpoint when compared to that of Rousseau. Like Rousseau he makes woman at once inferior and morally better, equates her good qualities with those of more primitive races, and apologizes for man's civilized behaviour, his regrettable ambition, with a self-satisfied smirk. He then tries to account for these ideas within the evolutionary framework. If evolutionary theory turned the world of the noble savage upside down, two men could apply utterly contradictory ideas to the same end when it came to justify-ing a familiar world that they recognized and had no wish to see changed. So Darwin ascribed the 'difference in mental powers' between men and women to a process of sexual selection, since the bravest, strongest and most resourceful men would acquire the most beautiful and healthy women:

With social animals, the young males have to pass through a contest before they win a female, and the older males have to retain their females by renewed battles. They have also, in the case of a man, to defend their females, as well as their young, from enemies of all kinds, and to hunt for their joint subsistence. But to avoid enemies, or to attack them with success, to capture wild animals, and to invent and fashion weapons, requires the aid of the higher mental faculties, namely, observation, reason, invention, or imagination. These various faculties will thus have been continually put to the test, and selected during manhood; they will, moreover, have been strengthened by use during this same period of life. Consequently, in accordance with the principle often alluded to, we might expect that they would at least tend to be transmitted chiefly to the male offspring at the corresponding period of manhood.

The last line is surprisingly tentative after such a long build-up, and no wonder. He seems to be flirting with the notion that all positive, 'masculine' characteristics are genetically sex-linked, one feels that he is trying to imply this without baldly stating an idea which he knows to be untenable. Scientific honesty eventually forces him to concede that

> With mammals the general rule appears to be that characters of all kinds are inherited equally by the males and females; we might therefore expect that with mankind any characters gained through sexual selection by the females would commonly be transferred to the offspring of both sexes.

Precisely. Incidentally, it is interesting to note that Darwin was typically a creature of his age in seeing the class and economic struggle as a continuation of the evolutionary one. Like Lecky he saw the maintenance of the *bourgeois* home as part of a more general social status:

> . . . although men do not now fight for the sake of obtaining wives, and this form of selection has passed away, yet they generally have to undergo, during manhood, a severe struggle in order to maintain themselves and their families; and this will tend to keep up or even increase their mental powers, and, as a consequence, the present inequality between the sexes.

The social order, with a living standard which involved economically dependent wives, was accepted without question. It does not appear to have occurred to either Lecky or Darwin that the 'severe struggle' could have been alleviated by ironing out rather than increasing the sexual inequalities, that the world they lived in was part of a social and economic process of change, and not the outer reality of an ultimate moral good. Thus Freud would not tolerate the idea of his fiancée finding work, and struggled on alone to attain his ideal of married life.

But the scientist trying to give logical foundation to his prejudice is on trickier ground than the moral historian. Lecky can trot out the usual clichés without giving them a second thought, and he does just that. 'Intellectually, a certain inferiority of the female sex can hardly be denied. . . . Women are intellectually more desultory and volatile than men; they are more occupied with particular instances than with general principles; they judge rather by intuitive perceptions than by deliberate reasoning . . . nimbleness and rapidity of thought . . . finer inflexions of feeling . . . often attained very great eminence in conversation, as letter-writers, as actresses, and as novelists. . . . Morally, the general superiority of women over men is, I think, unquestionable. . . . Men excel in energy, self-reliance, perseverance, and magnanimity; women in humility, gentleness, modesty, and endurance.' All the qualities of the industrious, competitive social animal on the one hand, and of the domesticated slave or pet on the other. But Darwin's attempts to prove these characteristics through evolutionary theory were doomed to failure, and he would have been better advised never to have made the attempt, which was inevitably both half-hearted and unconvincing. One is constantly aware that he himself is aware of skating on thin ice, and his words tend to tail off into tentative conjecture. 'No one will dispute that the bull differs in disposition from the cow,' he says, though he must have known that no one *was* disputing any such thing. But then no one is interested in the intellectual achievements of either bull or cow. Even on the question of womanhood's tenderness as a mother he quickly ties himself in knots. Like Rousseau, Darwin associates the characteristics of woman with those of more primitive races, and one of these is the capacity for tender solicitude as a parent. Conjecturing on primeval times, Darwin writes:

> At this early period the progenitors of man, from having only feeble powers of reason, would not have looked forward to distant contingencies. They would have been governed more by their instincts and even less by their reason than are savages at the present day. They would not at that period have partially lost one of the strongest of all instincts, common to all the lower animals, namely the love of their young offspring; and consequently they would not have practised infanticide.

Now, apart from the fact that as a naturalist Darwin must have been perfectly well aware that many lower animals not only kill but on occasion even eat their offspring, he also knew that not all women always conform to the required standard of motherhood. Although at one point he mentions woman's 'greater tenderness and less selfishness', proved (he says) by Mungo Park and other travellers, on another page we find him saying: 'In the Polynesian Islands women have been known to kill from four or five to even ten of their children; and Ellis could not find a single woman who had not killed at least one.'

Darwin's fundamental difficulties on the topic of man and woman stems from his inability to make any clear distinction between social conditioning and inherited tendencies. And for him there was a very real difficulty, since the social characteristics of man were part of his characteristics as an animal, i.e. man as he has emerged through the evolutionary process *is* a social animal, and has triumphed through his social instincts. 'There can be no doubt that a tribe including many members who, from possessing in a high degree the spirit of patriotism, fidelity, obedience, courage, and sympathy, were always ready to give aid to each other and to sacrifice themselves for the common good, would be victorious over most other tribes; and this would be natural selection.' There is an obvious over-simplification here, since 'patriotism' and a sheep-like willingness to die for the common good can also be the quickest road to self-destruction rather than survival. But nationalism and the family were twin gods of nineteenth-century morality and Darwin tended to see both as moral norms. Thus even nineteenth-century morality, with all its repression and hypocrisy, could be seen as 'inherited', and part of the evolutionary path to perfection:

> Looking to future generations, there is no cause to fear that the social instincts will grow weaker, and we may expect that virtuous habits will grow stronger, becoming perhaps fixed by inheritance. In this case the struggle between our higher and lower impulses will be less severe, and virtue will be triumphant.

It was left to Havelock Ellis, himself a believer in evolutionary progress as a form of change in the direction of what was naturally right and good, to give the prize in the evolutionary race to woman: since physiological change is in the direction of less body hair, a more delicate bone structure, less muscle and more brain in relation to body size, woman has obviously evolved further. She also, of course, lives longer. The question of brain characteristics, particularly size, is an interesting one: in relation to woman it appears to have obsessed nineteenth-century scientists, particularly German ones, much as it was later to obsess scientists who took skull measurements of murdered Jews under the Hitler régime, and for similar reasons. The fact that the male brain was larger was of course emphasized, and it was left to Havelock Ellis to point out that brain size has to be assessed in relation to body size, in which case woman actually wins the day. 'The history of opinion regarding cerebral sexual differences form a painful page in scientific annals,' he wrote, and gives an example:

> It was firmly believed that the frontal region is the seat of all highest and most abstract intellectual processes, and if on examining a dozen or two brains an anatomist found himself landed in the conclusion that the frontal region is relatively large in women, the probability is that he would feel he had reached a conclusion that was absurd. It may, indeed, be said that it is only since it has become known that the frontal region of the brain is of greater relative extent in the Ape than it is in Man, and has no special connection with the higher intellectual processes, that it has become possible to recognize the fact that the region is relatively more extensive in women.[1]

The bias is fundamental, and undermines not only theoretical sciences but the so-called objective ones, concerned with physical research and measurements. In fact, of course, there is no such thing as purely objective research, each man starts with a hypothesis, to be proved or abandoned. The great scientist is the man who does not merely abandon an unworkable and unprovable hypothesis, but can make a leap from one set of tracks to another, change horses in mid-stream, as it were. Intractable results prove something, if you can only make an imaginative leap rather than merely throwing the abortive experiment in the dustbin.

But the general run of men are stubbornly resistant to ideas that

[1] Havelock Ellis, *Man and Woman: A Study of Human Secondary Sexual Characters*.

undermine fundamental and familiar values, particularly those that undermine the pyramid. The idea that male supremacy was not founded on intrinsic merit was as unacceptable as the ideas of Galileo had once been to the medieval Church. Havelock Ellis gives an example of the prejudicial ability not just to twist the evidence, but to do a double twist in order to express one's own value judgments, which has a truly Swiftian flavour about it:

> The foot has received even more study than the hand, and certain interesting sexual differences emerge. Pfitzner, who has studied the foot with the same care as the hand, finds that there are two types of foot: the *elongated* type with long and well-developed middle phalanges, and the *abbreviated* type in which the middle phalanges are short and coarse. The first type is most common in men, the second in women. Which is the more primitive form? We are accustomed, he remarks, to regard women's forms as more primitive, but notwithstanding this he is inclined to look upon the abbreviated form common in women as a more recent acquisition of the race. At the same time he regards the abbreviated form as rather a retrogressive than a progressive evolution; 'no one can look at a middle phalanx of the abbreviated type and not recognise that it is unworthy of any noble mammal, and only to be regarded as *partie honteuse*.'[1]

The emotive aura of a human toe. One imagines Gulliver, caught in a war between male and female Lilliputians, arbitrating on the relative nobility of long and short toes.

In fact the evolutionary argument is a pointless one. It is a mistake to assume that change implies progress, or that survival is the only criterion. In the peacock evolution through sexual selection has produced perhaps the most beautiful bird known to man, but it cannot fly and would not survive outside a civilized park. The rational powers, the ability to think beyond the immediate contingency, which Darwin saw as leading to infanticide in the savage, have led to destructive powers which are probably not balanced by enough rational powers to think out the most distant contingencies of all. Even when man is being constructive, by trying to control his future environment for the future good of the species, by, for instance, genetic control of future generations, he may be destroying the species he is trying to improve by his

---

[1] Ibid.

inability to consider the most distant contingencies, his ignorance of all the facts. And in terms of ultimate survival a bloody war to reduce the population might be more effective than attempts at crop control, but this would not stop us from condemning one and applauding the other.

Man is a reasoning though not particularly reasonable animal. He lives in a world where he knows that he can gain a larger measure of control over material and living things than any other creature known to him, and yet he himself is infinitely small and vulnerable. It is natural that he should try to reassure himself by maximizing his own value and importance. New ideas have to be absorbed and internally transmuted so that they add to his image of himself rather than detract from it, build up and revitalize his sense of identity rather than to undermine and destroy it. Man's increasing awareness of his humble origins and basic, fundamentally animal nature was compensated for by a growing emphasis on mind, spirit, pure intelligence. The idea of Will, a kind of driving spirit propelling the vast evolutionary machine, became very important. It was through Will that man had begun to pull himself up and walk on two legs, it was Will that had made him paint the Sistine Chapel and build great cathedrals, it would be Will that sends him up into space. Nowadays we take a less romantic view and call it aggression. Although idealist philosophy was basically romantic and opposed to a materialistic and mechanistic view of the world, it ironically found its justification in the theory of evolution, since emotively one could read spirit into change, will into survival. Whether one thought in terms of a species, a race, a nation, or simply of the individual, no human aspirations were too high, and no sacrifice of those less fit or less aspiring need prove a moral deterrent if reaching a high ideal meant stepping on a ladder of necks. It was a romantic philosophy elaborated in Germany as theory during the nineteenth century, and put into practice by Hitler during the twentieth. Although fascism undoubtedly came into being as a result of political and economic factors, it is too often ignored that there was also a long tradition of intellectual thought, a climate both literary, artistic and philosophical, which appeared to justify such political attitudes. Naturally the Nazi party used words and ideas in a debased form for propagandist ends, but most politicians do this. The important point is that the bulk of the population found the coinage familiar and acceptable. Wagner was a musical genius, but he was also an anti-semite, and I do not know why people today should find this so difficult to digest, the whole climate of though favoured anti-semitism and a large majority of his contemporaries were anti-semitic. Even Tolstoy used the word 'Jew' as a rude word.

In the history of nineteenth-century German philosophy there is a distinct relationship between anti-semitism and anti-feminism, in the sense of hostility towards women and an emphasis on her general inferiority. It is no accident that the Third Reich made a concerted effort to reverse the trend towards female emancipation which had become general in Europe after the end of the First World War. The German woman was ordered back to the home, an attempt was made to exclude her from employment, and she was told that her proper interests in life were '*Kinder, Küche und Kirche*' (children, kitchen and church). The history of Germany not only shows one the dangers of romanticism, it proves that for all practical purposes one must treat people as fundamentally equal, and ignore the differences. John Stuart Mill defied his readers to find secondary sexual differences of character and ability which could be proved to be innate, and compared the slavery of women to that of negroes. A hundred years later no scientist has succeeded in conclusively refuting his contention. German writers elaborated theories on the different nature of woman and compared her to the Jew. The nation that was later to devote so much scientific effort to the skull measurements of murdered Jews was already specializing on trying to prove that women had inferior skulls and brains. Otto Weininger, the final flower of this philosophic line of thought, who wrote at great length on the foulness of women and the femininity of Jews, himself pointed out that there were only two systems of morality to choose from: he refers to the 'ethical socialism' of Bentham and Mill, and the 'ethical individualism such as is taught by Christianity and German idealism'. When we come to examine the latter we find that Parsifal's romantic woodland path leads, given the hands to build one, straight to the gas chamber.

If mind becomes the motor force of matter, it nevertheless implies a split, whereupon mind is extolled at the expense of matter. Just as earlier Christians distinguished between body and soul, and tended to portray woman as the incarnation of physical lust, the idealists also tended to make an evaluative split between mind and physical matter, with mind as male and the body, loathsome and sordid, as female. The male, particularly one who prizes his own intellectual abilities, is always trying to escape the demands of the body, which he regards as distracting and degrading, particularly his own sexual demands. An act of brutality, Strindberg called the sexual act, and Schopenhauer wrote: 'It is an action of which in cold reflection one generally thinks with dislike and in a lofty mood with loathing.'[1] The loathing is transferred to woman herself.

The total division of man as mind and woman as matter was to be expressed by Weininger at the end of the nineteenth century, but we can see the start of the process in Hegel's *Philosophy of Right*:

> In one sex the spiritual divides itself into two phases, independent, personal self-sufficiency, and knowing and willing of free universality. These two together are the self-consciousness of the conceiving thought, and the willing of the objective final cause. In the other sex the spiritual maintains itself in unity and concord. This sex knows and wills the substantive in the form of concrete individuality and feeling. In relation to what is without one sex exhibits power and mastery, while the other is subjective and passive. Hence the husband has his real essential life in the state, the sciences, and the like, in battle and in struggle with the outer world and with himself. Only by effort does he, out of this disruption of himself, reach self-sufficing concord. A peaceful sense of this concord, and an ethical existence, which is intuitive and subjective, he finds in the family. In the family the wife has her full substantive place, and in the feeling of family piety realizes her ethical disposition.

Hegel certainly does not deny woman her spiritual aspect, but Will in the idealist sense is a totally masculine affair. The man is active, the woman passive. In woman the physical and the mental are in perfect concord, do not war with each other, and this is in fact a

---

[1] *The World as Will and Idea*, Vol. 3, 'On the Assertion of the Will to Live'.

good description of animals as opposed to human beings, or, for that matter, of a cabbage. And the whole purpose behind this analysis is contained in the second part of this passage—a woman's place is in the home, and any alternative form of behaviour would put a woman in dire ethical peril and banish peace from the home. Civilization, the outward manifestation of the Will, is also masculine. 'Women can, of course, be educated, but their minds are not adapted to the higher sciences, philosophy, or certain of the arts. These demand a universal faculty. Women may have happy inspirations, taste, elegance, but they have not the ideal. . . . If women were to control the government, the state would be in danger, for they do not act according to the dictates of universality, but are influenced by accidental inclinations and opinions.' Since the dictates of universality were, for Hegel, a despotic form of German nationalism, its 'spirit' manifested in war and conquest, perhaps the least said about that the better.

Schopenhauer is by far the most attractive idealist philosopher, and there is a visionary coherence about his attitudes which makes one forgive him for much. He was of course a bitter misogynist, and found woman 'in every respect backward, lacking in reason and true morality . . . a kind of middle step between the child and the man, who is the true human being'.[1] He also mentions women's 'instinctive treachery, and their irremediable tendency to lying' and concludes that 'in the last resort, women exist solely for the propagation of the race'. But he tends to exonerate the female of the species on the grounds that she cannot help herself. His hatred of the sexual act has a logical as well as an emotional basis, in that the propagation of the species is highly undesirable. The whole awful machine should grind to a halt. If man is Will he would do far better if he could stop willing and die, but that is the one thing he cannot do. If woman is matter rather than spirit, her function to propagate the species, it would be far better if she did no such thing, but that is the one thing she cannot but do. Both men and women are duped by the illusion of love, hurled together by the sexual impulse, which is the will of the species to perpetuate itself. 'This impulse does away with carelessness, serenity, and innocence

[1] 'On Women'.

which would accompany a merely individual existence, for it brings unrest and melancholy into the consciousness; misfortunes, cares and misery into the course of life.'[1]

> The moment at which the parents begin to love each other . . . is really to be regarded as the first appearance of a new individual. . . . This new individual is to a certain extent a new (Platonic) Idea; and now, as all Ideas strive with the greatest vehemence to enter the phenomenal world, eagerly seizing for this end upon the matter which the law of causality divides among them all, so also does this particular idea of a human individuality strive with the greatest eagerness and vehemence towards its realisation in the phenomenon. This eagerness and vehemence is just the passion of the future parents for each other.[2]

Once the lover has got what he imagined he wanted, he inevitably feels cheated. And since 'the passion of love really turns about that which is to be produced', which is a constant attempt to return to a sort of Platonic ideal human being, people of opposite physique and characteristics are much more liable to fall in love in order to produce something approaching a reversal to the 'true type', and discord and incompatibility if marriage follows are inevitable.

If Schopenhauer was a misogynist with the misogynist's stereotyped views on womanhood, he was at least original in ascribing no blame to her for her infamous behaviour. If the male was the unwilling dupe of the species, she was the unwilling weapon. Women might incline to easy infidelity, but this was because they instinctively felt 'that by the breach of their duty to the individual, they have so much the better fulfilled that towards the species'.[3] If she was a deceitful hussy, this was because 'nature has armed woman with the power of deception for her protection'. As for the traps and taboos of nineteenth-century matrimonial morality, nature has also armed woman, if only 'for a few years', with

> superabundant beauty, fascination and fullness, at the cost of her whole remaining lifetime, in order that during these years she may be able to conquer the imagination of a man to the extent that he shall be so far carried away as to honourably undertake in some form or

[1] *The World as Will and Idea*, Vol. 3, 'On the Assertion of the Will to Live'.
[2] Ibid., 'The Metaphysics of the Love of the Sexes'.
[3] 'On Women.'

shape the care of her for life; a step for which more reasonable deliberation seems to give no adequate security.[1]

Love, woman, marriage, they are all traps laid for man who might otherwise live out his unhappy and pointless life in calm contemplation and thought. It all fits in with Schopenhauer's pessimistic view of the world. But now and then one detects a note of more personal vulnerability. In an essay on teleology in *The World as Will and Idea* he says that man was endowed with a beard in order to help him disguise changes of expression from an adversary. 'The woman, on the other hand, could dispense with this; for with her dissimulation and command of countenance are inborn.' Considering that he thought woman to be half-way between a child and a complete human being, she seems to have been far more richly endowed by nature for the battle of survival. Man, in fact, seems to do little but wait to be gobbled up, his function in life to impregnate woman and support her and her offspring for the rest of his life.

The idea of mind in control of matter implies some form of dominance; the concept of Will is soon transformed into a concept of Will to Power. Dominance is of course also the keynote in an analysis of the man–woman relationship where the male attributes are ones associated with mental thought and positive activity, whilst the woman is regarded as essentially passive, her role to be the receptacle of male sexual drive for the subsequent reproduction of the species. Thus Fichte, who as a philosopher glorified the subjective ego as the only reality, justified the patriarchal *status quo* in philosophical terms. Partial submission, he argues in *The Science of Rights*, would undoubtedly be humiliating, therefore a woman should submit totally to her man. 'In an uncorrupted woman the sexual impulse does not manifest itself at all, but only love; and this love is the natural impulse of a woman to satisfy a man.' Her role as the object of male sexual gratification demands a total abandonment, not only of all civil rights, but of her own personality. Woman has to be blind in love, since 'if woman ever should cease to regard in the man whom she satisfied the most lovable of all his

[1] Ibid.

sex, this thought alone would make her contemptible in her own eyes'. She might, is the implication, begin to suspect that she had given herself to a man for more earthly reasons than pure love, 'which would, doubtless, dishonour her in her own eyes'. And then somehow Fichte manages to glide quite imperceptibly from bedroom to more public rights:

> The woman who thus surrenders her personality, and yet retains her full dignity in so doing, necessarily gives up to her lover all that she has. For, if she retained the least of her own self, she would thereby confess that it had a higher value for her than her own person; and this undoubtedly would be a lowering of that person. Her own dignity requires that she should give herself up entirely as she is, and lives to her choice and should utterly lose herself in him. The least consequence is, that she should renounce to him all her property and all her rights. Henceforth she has life and activity only under his eyes and in his business. She has ceased to lead the life of an individual; her life has become a part of the life of her lover. (This is aptly characterized by her assuming his name.)

Thus honour requires dishonour, dignity demands total indignity, and freedom a willing slavery. A woman 'is subjected through her own continuous necessary wish—a wish which is the condition of her morality—to be so subjected'. Like Rousseau he condemns ambition in a woman, since it is inimical to the 'self-sacrificing love for her husband, upon which her whole dignity rests. A rational and virtuous woman can be proud only of her husband and children; not of herself, for she forgets herself in them'. Not only is honour based upon dishonour, her will (the symbol of power, and masculine power, for German philosophers of the nineteenth century) is to have no will:

> The state, by recognizing marriage . . . abandons all claims to consider woman as a legal person. The husband supplies her place; her marriage utterly annuls her, so far as the state is concerned, by virtue of her own necessary will, which the state has guaranteed.

Of course one does not need a training in philosophy or logic to realize that in order to will to have no will she must have had a will in the first place. In other words, in some peculiar form she did possess that fundamental masculine attribute. In requiring her to give it up, voluntarily of course, Fichte's thinking was very like that of another nineteenth-century patriarch. Freud, as we shall see later, demanded, not that woman should give up her will, but her masculinity, which in effect amounted to the same thing. And by saying that she had to renounce her masculinity at puberty, he was in fact admitting that her attributes as a human being were fundamentally similar to those of the male.

In Nietzsche the philosophy of Will becomes a hysterical shriek and we see the façade begin to crack. Too much emphasis on domination and superiority betrays fear and a profound insecurity. Unlike Schopenhauer's, Nietzsche's pose is affirmative. He does not regard the sexual act with loathing, on the contrary, he brags about sensuality as the natural relaxation of the 'warrior', and despises asceticism. 'Man should be trained for war and woman for the recreation of the warrior; all else is folly,' he writes in *Thus Spake Zarathustra*. He divides the world up into brave men and cowards, Romans and Jews, warriors and priests, to say nothing of men and women. His stance is always that of the tough warrior, but for him attack is really a means of defence. 'Are you visiting women? Do not forget your whip,' he remarks in *Zarathustra*, but the whip betrays quaking terror: 'The true man wants two things: danger and play. For that reason he wants woman, as the most dangerous plaything.' His attitude to woman is that of a lion-tamer entering a cage containing one of his big cats, even though he insists on her secondary role, and, indeed, the image is almost literally confirmed in *Beyond Good and Evil* where he says:

. . . man wishes woman to be peaceable: but in fact woman is essentially unpeaceable, like the cat, however well she may have assumed the peaceable demeanour.

Nietzsche divorces sexuality from emotion and adopts a hearty, swaggering tone, as though a relationship with a woman were rather like eating a large meal or having a drinking bout with the boys. And the reason for this is a fear of emotion. Under the pose of the swaggering warrior one can see a lack of assurance about the real nature of masculinity, resulting in falsely exaggerated aggression. It is one end product of sexual role playing, the man who has to try too hard to be a man, whose dominance disguises a vulnerability he dare not reveal. Nietzsche the superman not only fears woman but all the aspects of humanity which he associates with woman and which he affects to despise—gentleness, love, sympathy, suffering. He is afraid of these qualities and attempts to divorce them from himself, keep them at arm's length, because they undermine his strong pose. Since it is only a pose. In *A Genealogy of Morals* he spits scorn on 'that priestly people', the Jews, who 'dared to subvert the aristocratic equation of values (good=noble= powerful=beautiful=happy=beloved of God) and who, with the teeth of the profoundest hatred (the hatred of impotency), clung to their own valuation: The wretched alone are good; the poor, the impotent, the lowly alone are the good; only the sufferers, the needy, the sick . . .'. It is in fact a total rejection of Christianity, with its emphasis on humility and gentleness, on compliance to suffering. It is the Romans he admires, and detests the gentle Jews for undermining that strong empire; the Christian Jews, by 'a transvaluation of their values', managed to wreak a 'spiritual vengeance' on their Roman conquerors.

In Nietzsche, as in the man Hitler himself, we can see just how far hysterical domination, the emphasis on strong masculinity was based on fear:

> The sick are the greatest danger for the sound . . . the *sickly* are the great danger of man . . . they, the *weakest*, are those who most undermine life among men; who most dangerously poison and question our confidence in life, in man, in ourselves. . . . They walk among us like so many live reproaches, like so many warnings—just as if health, power, were, in themselves, vicious things which one day must be atoned for, bitterly atoned for. . . . The will of the sick to represent some form or other of superiority; their instinct for finding secret ways leading to a tyranny over the sound. . . . Sick woman especially; no one excels more in *raffinements*—of ruling, of oppressing, of tyrannising. A sick woman will spare nothing living, nothing dead; she will dig up the most deeply buried things.[1]

The terror of having to watch suffering, the man who runs away from a deathbed because he cannot bear his own tears, because he does not realize that to stay and suffer is more manly more courage-

[1] *A Genealogy of Morals.*

ous than to run away and renounce his ability to cry. The man who refuses to admit that no man is an island, that we are all mortal, of no account: 'Away with this shameful effeminacy of sentiment!' he goes on in *The Genealogy of Morals*:

> That the sick may *not* make the sound sick—and this would be the meaning of such effeminacy—surely, this should be the first point of view on earth. But for that the first condition is that the sound should be *removed* from the sick, guarded from the very aspect of the sick, that they may not confuse themselves with the sick.

The weak and sick should be cared for by those who are also weak and sick. But above all, no contamination, no hint of approaching incapacity or death. Ultimate escape may be impossible for the man posing as superman:

> But away, at any rate, from the foul vapours of internal corruption and the secret worm-eatenness of the sick!—In order that we, my friends, may guard ourselves, for some time at least, against the two most fatal plagues which may have been reserved just for us—against the *great surfeit of man* and the *great pity for man*.

It is an attitude which leads logically to the gas chamber built discreetly out of sight, the lunatic asylum where the inmates are simply wiped out.

Although the evaluative emphasis is different, Nietzsche like Rousseau saw pity and sympathy as feminine qualities, and ones that have little to do with masculine civilization. He condemns poets for just this quality of sympathy, and thinks that spurious characters like Byron, Musset, Poe, Leopardi, Kleist and Gogol must have acquired this fatal flaw from woman 'who is clairvoyant in the world of suffering, and also unfortunately eager to help and save to an extent far beyond her powers . . . woman would like to believe that love can do *everything*'.[1] But love, says Nietzsche, is blundering and helpless. Love does not save, it destroys. Nietzsche represents the kind of man who would shoot an injured dog, not to end the dog's suffering, but to end his own. Because he cannot bear to hear it whimper.

Just as the Christian Church had permitted sexuality within

[1] *Beyond Good and Evil*.

marriage for the procreation of the species, nineteenth-century moralists could only approve of sexuality within marriage. The family was regarded as the microcosm of the state, so that marriage was a way of maintaining the social order; the idealist could also regard it as a way of reconciling the opposing forces of mind and matter. Thus Kant wrote in his *Lectures on Ethics*:

> Matrimony is the only condition in which use can be made of one's sexuality. If one devotes one's person to another, one devotes not only sex but the whole person; the two cannot be separated.

Unfortunately real life is rarely as perfect or as simple as that, even within marriage, as Strindberg discovered. And for the young man who could not as yet afford marriage, in love with the idea of his own intellectuality, a prey to sexual temptation but trying all the while to prove the superiority of will and willpower, the domination of mind over matter, the demands of the body and woman who aroused those demands could prove a scourge. His problems were similar to those of the medieval saint fighting off the temptations of the devil.

The attitudes of such a young man are expressed by Otto Weininger, in whose book, *Sex and Character*, idealist thinking on the subject of women (with Jewry added as an appendix) came to full flower. Rather like Jung, whose thinking has more in common with German philosophy than with empirical science, Weininger starts with a supposition not unlike that of the animus and animal i.e. 'the existence of an ideal man, M, and of an ideal woman, W, as sexual types, although these types do not actually exist'. Men are male, and women are female, but all people have a touch of the opposite sex in them, and sometimes more than a touch. Jewish men have more than a touch of woman in them, and intellectual women or those who demand emancipation have a large proportion of maleness in their makeup. This was why George Sand used a male pseudonym and wore trousers, because 'some of the anatomical characters of the male' lurked under those velvet pants. George Sand was undoubtedly something of a freak. He also comments on George Eliot's large, masculine forehead. The beauty of this kind of approach is that it is infinitely adaptable, so that all exceptions can be made to prove the rule, and it requires neither science nor logic. You simply start with the proposition that to be male is to be positive, rational, active, dominating, and to be female is to be submissive, passive and not very bright, and no one can say you nay. A sliding scale of maleness and femaleness is simply applied to each individual case, and naturally it encourages conformity. Most women, about to have their femininity measured like a temperature, would prefer to doff velvet pants, down pens and go back to skirts and cookbooks, rather than have it thought that a hairy chest or male genitalia lurked under their unacceptable exteriors.

For Weininger the distinction between maleness and femaleness is only the groundwork for his main thesis: woman is matter, man is mind. Woman is a bundle of animal lusts, merely in the world for the purpose of procreation, whilst the life of man is something more, for man aspires to that pinnacle of idealist aspiration, Genius. Genius is conceived of in terms of idealist subjectivism:

> The genius is the man with the most intense, most vivid, most conscious, most continuous, and most individual ego . . . the external world in fact seems to be only a special aspect of his inner life; the universe and the ego have become one in him, and he is not obliged to set his experience together piece by piece according to the rule.

According to this definition he is undoubtedly liable to be a dangerous maniac. The female, Weininger states categorically, cannot be possessed of genius, she is little more than an animal: 'the life of the male is a more highly conscious life than that of the female', and 'there is not a single woman in the history of thought, not even the most manlike, who can be truthfully compared with men of fifth or sixth-rate genius'.

Having glorified genius as a masculine 'innate imperative', and expounded on the Kantian ethic that duty is merely duty to oneself, he comes to conclusions about the female which are surprisingly similar to those of the witch-hunter Sprenger. Pure woman equals total carnality, and for the absolute woman sexuality is the be-all and end-all of existence. Moreover:

> In such a being as the absolute female there are no logical and ethical phenomena, and, therefore, the ground for the assumption of a soul is absent. The absolute female knows neither the logical nor

the moral imperative, and the words law and duty, duty towards herself, are words which are least familiar to her. The inference that she is wanting in supersensual personality is fully justified. The absolute female has no ego.

Naturally she is also cunning, incapable of telling the truth, devoid of all notions of morality, beauty or even true mother love, and is totally 'under the sway of the phallus'. As his misogynist vituperation gathers momentum his internal philosophical logic becomes more and more wild. It is pointless to argue with him, he argues, since to include women in his definition of genius would simply be to change the definition of genius. Later on he has got to the stage of asserting that

> As the absolute female has no trace of individuality and will, no sense of worth or of love, she can have no part in the higher, transcendental life. The intelligible, hyper-empirical existence of the male transcends matter, space, and time. He is certainly mortal, but he is immortal as well.

From here it is but a step to Weininger's conclusion that:

> Women have no existence and no essence; they are not, they are nothing. Mankind occurs as male or female, as something or nothing. . . . The meaning of woman is to be meaningless. She represents negation, the opposite pole from the Godhead, the other possibility of humanity.

From the 'absolute woman' Weininger passes on to the 'absolute Jew', who is also devoid of a soul and, need I say it, 'womanish'. The true Jew is also incapable of genius. As a philosopher Weininger could hardly ignore Spinoza completely, so he condemns him for his rejection of the concept of free will—a truly Jewish thing to do, he says, since the Jew is always a slave and a determinist, like woman. 'Christ was a Jew, precisely that He might overcome the Judaism within him . . . he who has raised himself above the most desolate negation is most sure in his position of affirmation.'

But like the super-masculinity of Nietzsche, the affirmation of genius in Weininger was really based on unstable insecurity. At the age of twenty-three, because his male genius had not been sufficiently recognized on the publication of *Sex and Character*, Weininger killed himself.

The link between racism and anti-feminism should teach us a valuable lesson about the dangers of attempting to categorize people on the basis of physique—whether it is a matter of sex or skin colour. I am not of course saying that idealist philosophers would have condoned the Third Reich—even Otto Weininger, unbalanced as he was, disassociated himself from the idea of actively discriminating against Jews or women. He tended to feel that women being given civil rights would not really change the social situation—because her innate inferiority would prevent her making any constructive use of social equality. But this sort of attitude is undoubtedly the thin end of the wedge. There is a logical progression between saying that women are 'different' (really meaning inferior) to men, or that Jews or negroes are different to white Caucasians, and actually treating them as different. It soon becomes possible to deny such inferiors basic human rights, just as men denied woman a soul. The implication is that these inferiors are not human at all.

The Third Reich arose out of a political and economic situation, but Nazi politicians and propagandists undoubtedly found their justification in a philosophic jargon which was familiar to the German people. It was a government which was not only strongly anti-semite but strongly anti-feminist. As is always the case, of course, there were more practical reasons for taking this attitude. The German government found it convenient to say that woman's true place was in the home at a time of severe unemployment. If they idealized woman as wife and mother, she was rapidly turfed out of her kitchen once the war had started.

In a racist world, with an ideology based on the idea of aggression and conquest equated with Will and masculinity, woman's role as wife and mother was reinforced because she was required to propagate as fast as possible, both to provide cannon fodder and to populate the world with desirable Aryan stock. Aggression and the will to power being attributes only of the male sex, Dr. Goebbels could confidently say in 1934, when he explained why women should retire from public life and devote themselves exclusively to domestic affairs: 'The National Socialist movement is in its nature a masculine movement.'[1] Any German schoolboy who had read his Nietzsche knew that the Roman Empire was also masculine and that it was undermined by feminine Jews.

[1] Quoted by Clifford Kirkpatrick in *Woman in Nazi Germany*.

VI

Learning to be a Woman

We have suggested earlier on in this book that a patriarchal society depends on sexual taboos, and that psychological taboos have to be enforced with the decline of direct physical control. We see a modern example of this principle at work in an area of learning which, perhaps more than any other, has profoundly influenced our attitudes to ourselves and each other today. I refer to the teachings of Sigmund Freud, which came to full flower just when the social and economic dependency of women was being vigorously challenged. As women demanded the right to learn and work, to share in the capitalist system which men had come to regard as a natural male prerogative, Freudian analysis appeared on the intellectual horizon to provide a subtle psychological taboo: the would-be emancipated woman froze in her tracks, stopped from going further by a magic formula more powerful than any fence, and the psychological taboo which forbade her from venturing to compete still operates now.

We have already had occasion to refer to Freud's more personal, *ex cathedra* statements. We know that he took a dim view of John Stuart Mill's ideas on the unnatural subjection of women. We know that he himself was quite exceptionally monogamous, and appears to have been one of the few nineteenth-century men who actually lived up to the ideal of nineteenth-century morality. During a protracted engagement which involved prolonged separations he worked and studied hard, practised sexual restraint and saved money for the day when he and his little woman could move into their matrimonial nest. He sternly and fondly forbade his fiancée to so much as think of working herself, but the note of fondness in his letters to her, which are sprinkled with such endearments as 'sweet girl' and 'little princess', soon turns to obvious irritability if she shows signs of having a will of her own. He was particularly priggish when she chose to associate with a woman whom he considered to be not quite moral, or was reluctant to break off ties which made him jealous. After marriage he seems to have remained undisturbed by other women, to have found marriage a haven for the emotions, the right environment for a moral and hard-working man.

Freud was a child of his own times. Although he is popularly thought of as a revolutionary thinker who scandalized his own generation and shocked the nineteenth-century *bourgeoisie*, he was in fact thoroughly *bourgeois* himself and his theories are based on a total acceptance of the *status quo* as a norm of civilized behaviour. He might indicate the storms beneath the smooth exterior, recognize that the morality of his own society resulted in neurosis, but this did not stop him from subscribing to that morality. On the contrary. In Freud's work the emphasis is on the superego, on a conscious restraint of libidinous demands in the interests of civilization, and the values of the civilization he understood were thoroughly middle class: he did not doubt that marriage should be faithful and monogamous, that a father should be absolute head of his family, that industriousness, hard work and a lack of self-indulgence, particularly sexual, were qualities that should be cultivated. Neurosis was a regrettable but inevitable by-product of civilization, the price that had to be paid.

The one serious criticism that must be levelled at Freud time and again is his inability to see beyond the immediate social situation, so that he is constantly confusing cause and effect, his obstinate refusal to recognize that his own present day was itself transitional. His mentality was basically conservative and traditionalist, in many ways he was a diehard. In 1883, as a young man, forty-seven years before the publication of *Civilization and Its Discontents*, we find him writing to Martha Bernays:

> The mob gives vent to its appetites, and we deprive ourselves. We deprive ourselves in order to maintain our integrity, we economise in our health, our capacity for enjoyment, our emotions; we save ourselves for something, not knowing for what. And this habit of

constant suppression of natural instincts gives us the quality of refinement. We also feel more deeply and so dare not demand much of ourselves . . . we strive more towards avoiding pain than towards seeking pleasure. . . . Our whole conduct of life presupposes that we are protected from the direst poverty and that the possibility exists of being able to free ourselves increasingly from social ills. The poor people, the masses, could not survive without their thick skins and their easy-going ways. Why should they take their relationships seriously when all the misfortune nature and society have in store threatens those they love? Why should they scorn the pleasure of the moment when no other awaits them? The poor are too helpless, too exposed, to behave like us. When I see the poor indulging themselves, disregarding all sense of moderation, I invariably think that this is their compensation for being a helpless target for all the taxes, epidemics, sicknesses, and evils of social institutions. I am not going to pursue this thought any further, but it would be easy to demonstrate how 'the people' judge, think, hope and work in a manner utterly different from ourselves.[1]

This was how Freud justified the long years of a frustrating engagement to his intended bride. The middle-class morality of the nineteenth century was highly hypocritical, but Freud, like so many intellectuals before and since, made life difficult for himself by taking the ideals seriously and actually living up to them.

Freud's whole theory of civilization is based on the narrow world he lived in, and ironically, sexual demands both provided the foundation stone and constantly threatened to undermine the whole structure. The whole purpose of a civilized form of life was a fair share-out of the available women (for which we could read monogamy, marriage as Freud understood it) but its continuation depended on a renunciation of instinctual demands. Not only must we not be too greedy, by encroaching on another male's preserves, but we must learn to postpone immediate gratification for work, replace the pleasure principle with the reality principle. This, in a new language, is a reflection of a nineteenth-century morality that extolled hard work and sexual restraint, and advised its ambitious young men to postpone marriage until they were sufficiently established in a profession or industry to bring up a family in middle-class comfort. Civilization is and must be repressive. 'Every

[1] *Letters of Sigmund Freud*, p. 65.

individual is virtually an enemy of civilization,' Freud wrote in *The Future of an Illusion*, and:

> We know that a human child cannot successfully complete its development to the civilized stage without passing through a phase of neurosis sometimes of greater and sometimes of lesser distinctness. This is because so many instinctual demands which will later be unserviceable cannot be suppressed by the rational operation of the child's intellect but have to be tamed by acts of repression. . . .

But a large majority of people never become sufficiently repressed and/or civilized. The class distinctions made in that early letter to Martha Bernays are reiterated: 'It is just as impossible to do without control of the mass by a minority as it is to dispense with coercion in the work of civilization. For masses are lazy and unintelligent; they have no love for instinctual renunciation. . . . It is only through the influence of individuals who can set an example and whom masses recognize as their leaders that they can be induced to perform the work and undergo the renunciations on which the existence of civilization depends.'[1]

So civilization depends on a small, determined *élite* who are ruled by the reality principle rather than the pleasure principle. And this *élite* was undoubtedly totally masculine. Time and again, throughout his work, we find Freud saying that woman has little or no superego, that she is unable to renounce her instinctual demands. In *Civilization and Its Discontents* he goes further: woman not only did not assist in the work of civilization, which Freud saw as an all-male achievement, but was a downright hindrance:

> . . . women soon come into opposition to civilization and display their retarding and restraining influence—those very women who, in the beginning, laid the foundations of civilization by the claims of their love. Women represent the interests of the family and of sexual life. The work of civilization has become increasingly the business of men, it confronts them with ever more difficult tasks and compels them to carry out instinctual sublimations of which women are little capable. Since a man does not have unlimited quantities of psychical energy at his disposal, he has to accomplish his tasks by making an expedient distribution of his libido. What he employs for cultural aims he to a great extent withdraws from women and sexual life. His

[1] *The Future of an Illusion.*

constant association with men, and his dependence on his relations
with them, even estrange him from his duties as a husband and father.
Thus the woman finds herself forced into the background by the
claims of civilization and she adopts a hostile attitude towards it.

It has been going on for a long time, and one can see the pattern
here: the woman waiting at home, complaining about the long
hours he spends at the office, that he does not have time to pay
attention to her, that he eats, sleeps and dreams work. So she
becomes a drag on him. 'I have to earn my living,' the tired
executive might answer irritably, 'there are plenty of other men
waiting to step into my shoes.' The demands of civilization, Freud
would answer loftily.

What is remarkable about this passage is Freud's refusal to
question the *status quo*. He realizes that a situation where man works
and woman sits at home produces friction, but he does not so much
as consider any alternative social set-up. Although he made repeated use of 'history' in one sense, referring to a conjectural primeval past in order to elaborate his theories, he was totally lacking
in a more immediate and actual historical sense, ignored the comparatively recent development of the capitalist society in which he
lived and which had been so largely responsible for the separate
male and female roles which he took to be fundamental, and never
separated social from psychological factors. In a very real sense he
appears to have subscribed to a view of human progress in which
the here and now was the ultimate goal, and seems to have excluded
any idea of further change beyond his own lifetime.

Thus the image of the primal father is fundamental, in his thinking, to the human condition, and the whole Oedipal situation is not
the result of historical factors, of a patriarchal pattern of society
with families headed by authoritarian fathers, but basic to human
nature. It is usual nowadays to think of the first societies as being
matriarchal, but for Freud the idea of the authoritarian male is so
absolute that he visualizes human society as fundamentally patriarchal. In *Moses and Monotheism* he puts forward the thesis that
matriarchy was preceded by a primal patriarchy, and that power
temporarily passed into the hands of women as a result of the
Oedipal parricide, when the primal father was deposed. At this

stage totemism became a father-substitute. But matriarchy was soon followed by the re-establishment of a patriarchal order, and 'the re-establishment of the primal father in his historic rights was a great step forward'. A Jew himself, Freud was following a long Hebraic tradition already familiar to us from the Old Testament, *Genesis* in particular. Man came first, then woman. The argument for a primal patriarchy is difficult to uphold and easily becomes tortuous. All those goddesses for example. 'It is likely', Freud explains, 'that the mother-goddesses originated at the time of the curtailment of the matriarchy, as a compensation for the slight upon the mothers. The male deities appear first as sons beside the great mothers and only later clearly assume the features of father-figures.' Surely no one could swallow this explanation, not only does it shrink history to the dimensions of a parlour game, but Freud would have us believe that goddesses were invented as a form of compensation to aggrieved ladies. This is nonsense, goddesses, like all deities, embody authority and belief. Otherwise one might as well declare that the Hebraic masculine god, or any male god, for that matter, was an attempt to compensate the men of a community for some real or imagined slight. Which is not only absurd, but would have shocked the manly Freud to the core.

Although Freud did of course repudiate religion, one might say that by implication, at least, he approved the Hebraic monotheistic tradition which had been part of both Jewish and Christian teaching for so long, because for him it embodied absolutes of the human psyche, because like civilization itself (of which it was a stage) the Judaic-Christian religion was authoritarian, repressive of instinctual demands, and patriarchal. One could say that Freud rejected the superstition but retained the moral code. There may be no God, is his attitude, but we have to have a primal father figure, or chaos results. Thus Freud condoned his own civilization. Matriarchy, with its lack of sexual repression and the importance accorded to women, had to be regarded as a temporary liberation, the result of parricide, from the right and natural despotism of the primal father, without which civilization could go no further.

When we turn from the general to the particular, from Freud's broad concepts of civilization to his particular analysis of the male and female psyche we can see just how profoundly his patriarchal attitude conditioned his 'findings'. If man had to give up instinctual demands in the interests of human civilization, that was nothing compared to the psychic sacrifices required of woman. Every woman, Freud is in fact saying, is a square peg trying to fit into a round hole, but since there are nothing but round holes it is necessary for the corners to be knocked off.

We must always bear in mind, whilst considering Freud, a fact of which Freud himself was not sufficiently aware: namely, that he was studying the human psyche, and neurosis in particular, at a time when life for women was quite extraordinarily stultifying, to a degree it has never been before or since in European history. But, as we have remarked before, a historical and social sense was not Freud's strong point.

In his biography of Freud, Ernest Jones wrote that he regarded women 'as having their main function to be ministering angels to the needs and comforts of men. His letters and love choice make it plain that he had only one type of sexual object in his mind, a gentle feminine one. While women might belong to the weaker sex, however, he regarded them as finer and ethically nobler than men'.[1] This is an attitude we have already analysed, it remained in force throughout the nineteenth century, but it does not augur well for the founder of psycho-analysis. And, indeed, Ernest Jones goes on: 'There is little doubt that Freud found the psychology of women more enigmatic than that of men. He said once to Marie Bonaparte: "The great question that has never been answered and which I have not yet been able to answer, despite my thirty years of research into the feminine soul, is *What does a woman want?*".'

Since he had never thought to ask her what she wanted, since his whole life and work had been devoted to telling her what she should want, the fact that woman should have remained an enigma is hardly surprising. And, of course, one of the results of the sexual role-playing which both Freud and society as a whole encouraged, is that most women, even if asked, would no longer really know

[1] Ernest Jones, *The Life and Work of Sigmund Freud*, p. 377.

141

what they wanted, or would want what they had been told to want. It is like the repressive parent who shouts at his child: 'Do not argue with me, do as you are told' and then, when the child becomes dull and sulky, silent and moody, shrugs his shoulders and complains to a neighbour: 'I don't know what's the matter with him. What does he want?' The more strongly patriarchal a society, the more there will be a tendency for a mystique of womanhood, for women to be regarded as something of an enigma. As late as 1933 Freud, pioneer explorer of the human mind, opened a lecture on 'Femininity' with the words:

> Throughout history people have knocked their heads against the riddle of the nature of femininity. . . . Nor will *you* have escaped worrying over this problem—those of you who are men; to those of you who are women this will not apply—you are yourselves the problem.

Freud's ideas on feminine psychology all spring from the tenet that woman's role in life is to stay at home, be passive in relation to man, bear and raise children. For instance, take Freud's very curious theory of female sexual excitation, still widely propagated by neo-Freudians today, and one that must have caused considerable unnecessary neurosis in many a modern woman. According to this theory sexual interest in the female child is focused on the clitoris, but later on sexual sensation is transferred to the vagina, so that the woman can fulfil her adult function of childbearing. This is the reality principle taking over from the pleasure principle with a vengeance. The clitoris is associated, not only with the idea of a masculine penis, which must be given up, but with pure pleasure, with masturbation. The vagina serves a childbearing function, and we know that in the nineteenth century 'uncorrupted', decent women were not supposed to want sexual gratification, only babies. The idea of 'giving up' the clitoris is Freud's expression of a repressive, male-orientated morality. If woman feels pleasure at all, it must be in one area only, that associated with childbearing. The clitoris is associated with the penis, with the active masculine role, and gives sexual pleasure. The vagina is passive and feminine, and produces babies. As Kinsey remarked, many women are seriously disturbed by their inability to make the transference, and even Freud realized that there were difficulties, that sometimes 'the clitoridal zone refuses to abandon its excitability'.[1] If a woman does not succeed in making the transference, in assuming her adult role, when 'the wish for a penis is replaced by one for a baby'[2] frigidity and neurosis are the result. But at the same time Freud was forced to admit, that 'the clitoris, with its virile character, continues to function in later female sexual life in a manner which is very variable and which is certainly not yet satisfactorily understood. We do not', he went on, 'know the biological basis of these peculiarities in women; and still less are we able to assign them any teleological purpose.'[3] As a result he hesitantly adopted a theory of bisexuality, which 'comes to the fore much more clearly in women than in men',[4] which he confessed to be confused and contradictory, and which would not fit in with his theory of instincts.

But these moments of doubt are relatively rare. On the whole Freud sticks rigidly to his principle that civilization means the renunciation of instinctual demands, and that neurosis is simply an unfortunate but inevitable by-product. The fact that there are more casualties amongst the female sex is put down to her curious biological make-up, and not to the fact that a male-orientated society may demand too many renunciations of woman:

> When erotogenic susceptibility to stimulation has been successfully transferred by a woman from the clitoris to the vaginal orifice, it implies that she has adopted a new leading zone for the purpose of her later sexual activity. A man, on the other hand, retains his leading zone unchanged from childhood. The fact that women change their leading erotogenic zone in this way, together with the wave of repression at puberty, which, as it were, puts aside their childish masculinity, are the chief determinants of the greater proneness of woman to neurosis and especially to hysteria. These determinants, therefore, are intimately related to the essence of femininity.[5]

Women must give up their 'childish masculinity'. The idea of role-playing is very strong in Freud's work. In *Civilization and Its Discontents*, for example, he admits that the association between masculinity and activity, femininity and passivity is not universally borne out by the animal kingdom, and that the theory of

[1] 'Female Sexuality' (1931).   [2] 'Femininity' (1933).
[3] 'Female Sexuality'.   [4] Ibid.   [5] Ibid.

bisexuality, with which he seems to have been more and more preoccupied at the time as an escape clause (also cautiously mooted in his essay on 'Female Sexuality' published a year later, in 1931) 'is still surrounded by many obscurities and we cannot but feel it is a serious impediment in psycho-analysis that it has not yet found any link with the theory of instincts'. But, he concludes:

> if we assume it as a fact that each individual seeks to satisfy both male and female wishes in his sexual life, we are prepared for the possibility that those [two sets of] demands are not fulfilled by the same object, and that they interfere with each other unless they can be kept apart and each impulse guided into a particular channel that is suited to it.[1]

As we have pointed out in a previous chapter, a theory of bisexuality is the ultimate escape hatch for anyone who wishes to ascribe particular characteristics to either sex. So, just as Otto Weininger could remark that any attempt to allow for the inclusion of women among geniuses would simply change the definition of genius, Freud could also remark jovially, in his lecture on 'Femininity', that any feminist objection to his ideas could be met on the grounds of bisexuality, with the polite answer: 'This doesn't apply to *you*. You're the exception; on this point you're more masculine than feminine.'

However, Freud certainly did not consider it desirable for a woman's masculine traits to remain unsuppressed. If they did she was liable to become neurotic, frigid, thoroughly dangerous to her husband, and might try to compete with males in intellectual pursuits. In any case, for all girls penis-envy is as basic a trauma as the castration complex is for boys.

Once again one is faced with Freud's lack of a historical sense. In a society not sexually repressive little boys would be unlikely to develop castration fears; in a society where all the material rewards did not go to those endowed with penises there would be no natural envy of that regalia. We know why blacks try to whiten their skins. But more important, Freud himself is really convinced that women lack something, that there is something missing, rather like the psycho-analyst who reassures his patient with the words:

[1] *Civilization and Its Discontents.*

144

'Don't worry, you do not have an inferiority complex, you *are* inferior.' It is when a woman refuses to accept this state of affairs, rebels against her inevitable lot, that the trouble really starts. When men reach adult life, all that is left of the castration complex is 'a certain amount of disparagement in their attitude towards women, whom they regard as being castrated',[1] but: 'Quite different are the effects of the castration complex in the female. She acknowledges the fact of her castration, and with it, too, the superiority of the male and her own inferiority; but she rebels against this unwelcome state of affairs.'[2]

> The wish to get the longed-for penis eventually in spite of everything may contribute to the motives that drive a mature woman to analysis, and what she may reasonably expect from analysis—a capacity, for instance, to carry on an intellectual profession—may often be recognized as a sublimated modification of this repressed wish.[3]

In a paper highly praised by Freud, Karl Abraham puts forward the same view of female ambition as a manifestation of the castration complex. 'A considerable number of women', he writes, 'are unable to carry out a full psychical adaption to the female sexual role.' In this case the women may become homosexual, but:

> In some cases their homosexuality does not break through to consciousness; the repressed wish to be male is here found in a sublimated form in the shape of masculine pursuits of an intellectual and professional character and other allied interests. Such women do not, however, consciously deny their femininity, but usually proclaim that these interests are just as much feminine as masculine ones. They consider that the sex of a person has nothing to do with his or her capacities, especially in the mental field. This type of woman is well represented in the woman's movement of today.[4]

So homosexuality disguised as intellect is one consequence of the failure to take what Freud called the 'very circuitous path' to the 'normal female attitude'.[5] Another possible consequence was frigidity.

Now until very recently sexual frigidity in women was un-

---

[1] 'Female Sexuality'.   [2] Ibid.   [3] 'Femininity'.
[4] 'The Female Castration Complex' (1920) from *Selected Papers of Karl Abraham M.D.* (Hogarth Press, 1927).
[5] 'Female Sexuality'.

doubtedly a very real problem, thanks to the unnatural restraints imposed upon them for so long. But when one reads Freud and, for that matter, Karl Abraham, one cannot help feeling that both analysts were more concerned with male discomfiture than with female unhappiness. 'Frigidity', wrote Abraham in the essay quoted above, 'is a form of aggression against the man by disappointing him', and anyone who has read Freud's 'The Taboo of Virginity'[1] cannot but be struck by the awful dangers that await the unfortunate male in the bedroom.

'Sexual thraldom' (meaning the psychological dependency which we associate with being in love) is necessary, says Freud in this essay, for the maintenance of civilized, monogamous marriage. It is far more common in women than in men and largely depends on the fact of a girl being a virgin at the time of her marriage. The thraldom is enforced by defloration. But the act of defloration can arouse a deep hostility in the woman towards her sexual partner, women have even been known to attack their husbands after coitus and this hostility can last as long as the marriage; which is why, says Freud, second marriages are often so much more successful. True to his habit of ignoring historical and sociological factors, this hostility is not ascribed by Freud to a combination of male clumsiness on the one hand, and unnaturally prolonged ignorance and chastity on the other, but firstly to a continuation of 'immature sexuality', i.e. the father fixation ('A husband is, so to speak, never anything but a proxy') and secondly to a much more deep-seated hostility, the result of penis envy, the woman's refusal to fulfil her feminine function. When one imagines the orthodox disciple of Freud in his bedchamber, refusing to acknowledge the function, teleological or otherwise, of his wife's clitoris, one can understand the nervous preoccupation with frigidity. But Freudian feminine psychology, with its emphasis on female passivity in general and exclusively vaginal excitation in particular, must have caused more frigidity than it ever cured.

The idea of the male superego is authoritarian, punitive and repressive. It is fallacious if only because no civilization could make

[1] *Collected Papers*, Vol. IV.

any progress through a body of males who had learned to conform to their elders' values through the fear of castration—progress depends on adventure, the original mind has to break away from the values of the previous generation. By saying that man gave up his instinctual demands and woman did not, Freud was in fact over-simplifying the nature of those demands. Men do not give up or postpone physical gratifications out of a sense of social responsibility—they enjoy, if not the work itself, the money and power that work gives. In other words, social action is in itself an important form of gratification: the man who leaves for his office at nine o'clock in the morning would not prefer to make love at that moment. There is a time and place for that as well.

In actual fact it was woman who was giving up her instinctual demands, not only the demand for full sexual enjoyment but the demand for freedom and variety of action. As I said earlier, Freud's basic view was that every woman was a square peg trying to fit into a round hole. It did not occur to him that it might be less destructive to change the shape of the holes rather than to knock all the corners off. The saddest indictment of this system is given by Freud himself. He concluded his essay on 'Feminity' by saying:

> . . . I cannot help mentioning an impression that we are constantly receiving during analytic practice. A man of about thirty strikes us as a youthful, somewhat unformed individual, whom we expect to make powerful use of the possibilities of development opened up to him by analysis. A woman of the same age, however, often frightens us by her psychical rigidity and unchangeability. Her libido has taken up final positions and seems incapable of exchanging them for others. There are no paths open to further development; it is as though the whole process had already run its course and remains thenceforward insusceptible to influence—as though, indeed, the difficult development to femininity had exhausted the possibilities of the person concerned. As therapists we lament this state of things, even if we succeed in putting an end to our patient's ailment by doing away with her neurotic conflict.

The 'cured' patient is actually brainwashed, a walking automaton, as good as dead. The corners have been knocked off and the woman accepts her own castration, acknowledges herself inferior, ceases to envy the penis and accepts the passive role of femininity. Sadly, man recognizes that the ideal, submissive woman he has created for himself is somehow not quite what he wanted.

Of all the factors that have served to perpetuate a male-orientated society, that have hindered the free development of women as human beings in the Western world today, the emergence of Freudian psycho-analysis has been the most serious. The fact that theoreticians have since split into a dozen schisms, that Freudian theory has been adapted and large parts of it rejected by some analysts since is only important in a strictly clinical situation (and not always then), it is Freud that most people read and know about. Psycho-analysis, whatever individual therapists may say, does tend to encourage conformity which may amount to something like brainwashing. If you are unhappy, the tendency is not to look at your situation and change that, you look within yourself and try to adapt yourself to the situation.

Many analysts have taken issue with Freud and rejected the idea of female inferiority, which they see as the result of a social situation. But the fact is that, not only are there still many orthodox Freudians practising and writing, but Freudian ideas have also become very popular currency. Any woman who fails to achieve orgasm on occasion, who discovers that she does not love her husband as much as she feels she ought, or who finds that she does not want to start a family or is not as involved with her children as society tells her she should be, is liable to worry about whether she is in some way rejecting her own femininity. And, ironically, as some theoreticians reject the Freudian theory of instincts and concentrate more on environmental factors and the care of children, the onus of motherhood appears to become heavier, at least in the imagination of the mothers. Instead of children being encouraged to early self-reliance and independence, an over-protective form of mothering has emerged in the West. Even though Dr. Spock himself has remarked on the fact that the children of working mothers in Russia do not appear to have those little nervous disorders so common amongst American children, even though research appears to confirm that the children of working mothers do better at school, are less nervous and are subject to less family conflict, research also reveals that almost all mothers who do go out to work feel guilty about it. The fact that children need security and a regular way of life has been generally interpreted as meaning that the child's physical mother must always be at hand.

The cult of Freudian femininity is by no means dead—one might almost say that it is the last bastion of the institution of marriage. After all, if both partners in a marriage consider their own wishes and interests as equally important conflict is bound to arise. A study made in 1963[1] found that marital satisfaction was related to the wife's ability to perceive her husband's expectations. Their happiness was not correlated with the husband's perception of the wife's expectations, or with their agreement on various aspects of family living. In other words, someone has to be the boss, and it ought to be the man. So a woman's femininity is still defined in terms of her plasticity with regard to man. The predominant trait of the feminine woman, wrote Helene Deutsch, is eroticism.[2] Which is just another way of saying that she is primarily a sexual object. 'What is common to all these [feminine] types is facility in identifying with man in a manner that is most conducive to the happiness of both partners. . . . To the woman falls the larger share of the work of adjustment: she leaves the initiative to the man and out of her own need renounces originality.' For Helene Deutsch, a traditional Freudian, these are the 'good' women, what she calls 'ideal life companions for men'—'They are the loveliest and most unaggressive of helpmates and they want to remain in that role; they do not insist on their rights—quite the contrary. They are easy to handle in every way—if one only loves them.' The 'bad' women are people like George Sand, who, she said, 'led a very promiscuous life and ruined many men'. 'Each of George Sand's numerous love affairs terminated in literally the self-same catastrophe: the man was destroyed.'[3] Surely a gross distortion of the true facts. But it is really her intellectuality, which she calls 'a kind of refuge from disappointments in love' which Deutsch cannot forgive. Intellectual activity in woman is a sublimation of the masculinity complex, successful women in this field 'are

---

[1] *The Development of Sex Differences*, edited by Eleanor E. Maccoby, pp. 211-12.
[2] Helene Deutsch, *Psychology of Women*, Vol. 1, p. 151.   [3] Ibid., p. 235.

not aware of the fact that they have paid a high price for it in their feminine values. Woman's intellectuality is to a large extent paid for by the loss of valuable feminine qualities: it feeds on the sap of the affective life and results in impoverishment of this life . . . intuition is God's gift to the feminine woman; everything relating to exploration and cognition, all the forms and kinds of human cultural aspiration that require a strictly objective approach, are with few exceptions, the domain of the masculine intellect, of man's spiritual power, against which woman can rarely compete. All observations point to the fact that the intellectual woman is masculinized; in her, warm intuitive knowledge has yielded to cold unproductive thinking'.[1] And she goes on to say that the masculinized woman does not really achieve anything original but simply exploits masculine achievement. 'She likes to show her identification with men, but unlike the feminine woman, she proposes to do so not by intuitive sympathy, but by a kind of shrewd grasp of masculine ideas and a flattering appreciation of them.' Familiar echoes of Rousseau. 'They can pick up a little of everything, I daresay,' said Mr. Stelling, when Tom Tulliver asked his tutor whether girls could do Euclid. 'They've a great deal of superficial cleverness; but they couldn't go far into anything. They're quick and shallow.' George Eliot was speaking ironically, since the heart of the tragedy in *The Mill on the Floss* is the fact that Maggie was deprived of an education that would have benefited her, an education that was quite unsuitable for her brother, whose real interests were practical. But Helene Deutsch is speaking in deadly earnest. Male dominance can only work with the connivance of the women of a society, and taboos must have their psychological effect on everyone in order to work; but the fact that women themselves (and educated specialists at that) should perpetuate the cult of the womanly woman to this extent is surely proof, not only of the powerful influence of Freud, but of the conformist tendencies which exist at an intellectual as well as a social level: reasoning is shaped by our attitudes, and not vice versa. The outlook is alarming when the conformist is a therapist. The power of such ideas is alarming because it affects both the sick and the

[1] Ibid., pp. 229–30.

healthy, it affects the way we educate people both at home and at school. The people who give marriage guidance are affected by it—I opened a book on one of the foremost marriage guidance services in this country and the first words that caught my eye was a description of one of the female clients: *Accepts femininity sexually, but tries to behave as a man in other respects.* What in god's name is this supposed to mean? The book was published in 1968.[1] That particular patient became increasingly depressed and eventually suicidal, according to the follow-up reports. A leucotomy was even considered. The patient had originally arrived with depression and a confused attitude to her own femininity, which the therapist was trying so unsuccessfully to stabilize. The victims of our social way of life are being treated with a double dose of the disease which originally struck them down—the inadequate brainwashing of childhood is reinforced with a course of therapy when those who break down come for help. There is always a price to be paid for social adjustment, but the price being paid for marital stability is often far too high. It is being paid for by both men and women but, since we live in a male-dominated society, women are by and large paying the higher price. We may become aware of it when there is unhappiness, neurosis and breakdown, but none of us will ever really know just how many corpses are walking about, people who are spiritually dead and defeated, people whose lives are one big might-have-been.

---

[1] M. Courtenay, *Sexual Discord in Marriage* (Tavistock Publications, 1968).

VII

A Woman's World

As Freud remarked, throughout history men have knocked their heads against the riddle of the nature of femininity. As for women, well, they were themselves the problem. 'Have you any notion how many books are written about women in the course of one year?' Virginia Woolf asked her audience of girl students in *A Room of One's Own*. 'Have you any notion how many are written by men? Are you aware that you are, perhaps, the most discussed animal in the universe?'

We have explored the discussion over the past two thousand years, if such one-sided dogmatism can be called discussion at all. All the assertions have been expressed by men, and for obvious reasons. Not because woman was herself the problem, not because only man could crack the nut of the riddle of femininity, but simply because woman had no say in the matter. Not in public, at any rate, and not for the record. We have no doubt that in private she always had plenty to say, which is one of the reasons that 'a woman's tongue' has always been considered a particularly dreadful scourge by the male. Whilst the Church was still powerful many sermons were preached against the wagging of female tongues, as well as vanity and idleness. The masculine ideal of womanhood was portrayed in the patient Grizelda, who suffered gross injustice and never uttered one word of reproach.

Until very recent times woman had no public voice. She was excluded from education and public affairs. It is a vast black ocean of silence stretching back into the past. This is often taken as proof of woman's natural disinclination to public expression or action, her basic contentment with a traditional role. Up to a point I am not disputing this: most people do as much or as little as is expected of them; most people want only as much as they have been taught to regard as their right. Life in the past has been a good deal more brutish and short than it is even now, with few gleams of light for any but a tiny minority, regardless of sex. After the American Civil War many Southern slaves had no wish for a freedom they did not understand, and *Uncle Tom's Cabin* had to be written by a white woman, because no blacks had the education to produce such a work.

It is not until the eighteenth and, more particularly, the nineteenth century that self-expression amongst women became at all common, as a result of increased leisure and more widespread literacy. Almost as soon as there was a considerable minority of articulate women, feminism also reared its ugly head. A two-class system never works for long unless one can have a rigid apartheid, and that would hardly work between men and women. Rousseau pointed out that no civilized man would want to spend his whole life beside a total ignoramus. An attempt was made to confine woman's education to the pursuits of leisure, to the cultivation of 'good taste' and the arts, but the situation soon got out of hand. In an age of cheap printing reading alone can open up a whole new world, and it becomes difficult to control. Teach a peasant to read the Bible for his moral edification, and before you know where you are he has his nose buried in Karl Marx.

I do not want to spend time on the feminist movement as such. This is well documented and familiar history. Instead I thought I would spend a little time reading between the lines to discover what some of the better feminine minds thought about their situation as women, women who, for the most part, took no part in the feminist movement or deliberately held back from associating their names with it.

The young Queen Victoria was wholly under the tutoring influence of Lord Melbourne. 'No woman', Lord Melbourne is recorded as saying in Victoria's diary, 'ever wrote a really good book.'[1] And when she discussed her proposed marriage with him he told her: 'I think it is a very good thing, and you'll be much more

[1] Diaries of Queen Victoria, 1838.

comfortable; for a woman cannot stand alone for long, in whatever situation she is.' Imagine the young Elizabeth Tudor being advised along these lines! Monarchs not only fashion their age, but are fashioned by it, so that they can become a sort of personification of the age. If Elizabeth I, independent, strong, represents the age of Shakespeare's heroines, a woman's heyday, Victoria represents another image of womanhood, predominant in the nineteenth century: a woman who, although queen in her own right, leaned on her husband, looked up to him, and went into perpetual mourning after his death. The feminist movement filled her with shocked horror and outrage.

But in fact many women who achieved success in their own right were unsympathetic to militant feminism. George Eliot's dubious social position with regard to Lewes made her anxious to conform; she thought it more important to suffer than to insist upon one's rights. Her desire to condone conventional marriage and morality, combined with her real understanding of the limitations imposed on women, accounts for Maggie Tulliver's unnecessarily sacrificial end. George Eliot was very sensitive to the imputation that she had 'stolen' Lewes from his lawful wife. Like many intellectual women, she preferred the company of men to that of her own sex, whose conversation was largely confined to drawing-room trivia. Later Beatrice Webb (an élitist to the core) was to show herself hostile to the female suffrage movement, and declared at a public luncheon that she had never met a man, however inferior, 'whom I do not consider to be my superior'. But she was careful to avoid a brilliant marriage which would have kept her in the background. Caroline Norton, whose agitation led to early marriage law reform, wrote that she believed in 'the natural superiority of man, as I do in the existence of God. The natural position of woman is inferiority to man'.

Brilliant people, people who managed to break through a host of social and psychological impediments against all the odds and achieve something, are the sort who do not usually suffer fools gladly. And the society in which they lived produced women who *were* foolish, who *were* tedious in comparison to men. One of the reasons that exceptional people do not suffer fools gladly is simply the fact that they do not recognize anything exceptional in themselves. If I can do all this without civil rights, why can't you?

A good example of this state of mind is Florence Nightingale who, in later years, gave the assent of her famous name to feminist causes with great reluctance. 'I am brutally indifferent to the wrongs and rights of my sex,' she wrote to Harriet Martineau in 1858,[1] and it made her angry that women should agitate to become doctors when she could not recruit enough good nurses. Let them get on with the job in hand, there was more than enough work for willing hands and sensible brains. That for an intelligent, educated woman, nursing was not so much a career as a form of martyrdom, did not occur to her, or that others could lack her singlemindedness. She not only ignored the fact that her own spirit and determination were exceptional, she also rather arrogantly forgot that her own social position was out of the ordinary. She came from a wealthy family with powerful connections. All her life she had been able to get things done in the traditional fashion condoned by the other sex, 'through' men, but not through a husband who could be wheedled into buying the odd present or taking her to the ball; no, she wheedled and bullied powerful men behind the scenes, manipulated cabinet ministers and high officials with the force of her determined mind. You do not need the vote to do that, but you do need private connections, beauty and brilliance alone won't do the trick. And economically she was also independent. When her father realized that his daughter would never make a conventional marriage as he wished, he made her an allowance of £500 a year. Throughout her life Florence Nightingale never drew a salary, expenses and printing bills were frequently paid for out of her own pocket. As Virginia Woolf said, give me £500 a year and a room of my own, and you can keep the vote. Incidentally, Florence never managed to keep within the allowance.

But the life of Florence Nightingale before that allowance was made is quite another story. This is what I mean by reading between the lines—one must not take too much notice of the public dicta of a public female figure on the question of woman's rights. It is the private woman one must turn to.

[1] See Cecil Woodham Smith, *Florence Nightingale*.

Florence Nightingale was well over thirty years of age before her family abandoned all hope of persuading their elder daughter to make a conventional marriage. During that time she was emotionally disturbed to such an extent that she was frightened of going mad. She was prone to day-dreaming fantasies, like a moonstruck schoolgirl. She heard voices, like Joan of Arc, which promised her a mission from God, and waited year in, year out, for an elucidation on what the mission in life was to be. She wrote private notes in which she complained about the dreadfulness of her woman's lot, and even published a novel on this theme, which she had privately printed and distributed amongst her friends. She hated being constantly at the beck and call of her family, unable to apply her mind to anything consistent. The woman who later declared herself 'brutally indifferent to the wrongs and rights of my sex' also wrote: 'Women don't consider themselves as human beings at all. There is absolutely no God, no country, no duty to them at all, except family . . . I know nothing like the petty grinding tyranny of a good English family.' And on another occasion she noted: 'I see so many of my kind who have gone mad for want of something to do.'

All this in spite of the fact that Florence Nightingale had both the opportunity and the ability to make the most of life. As a young woman she could enjoy travel and parties, and her private fantasies were not the result of sexual frustration. She was no ugly duckling, and there were suitors to choose from. One in particular courted her for many years, and she loved him. She noted down her reasons for refusing to marry Richard Monckton Milnes:

> I have an intellectual nature which requires satisfaction and that would find it in him. I have a passionate nature which requires satisfaction and that would find it in him. I have a moral, an active nature which requires satisfaction and that would not find it in his life. Sometimes I think I will satisfy my passional nature at all events, because that will at least secure me from the evil of dreaming. But would it? I could be satisfied to spend a life with him in combining our different powers in some great object. I could not satisfy this nature by spending a life with him in making society and arranging domestic matters.

Making society and arranging domestic matters, a mere continuation of the frustrating life she had known so far. Once she was allowed to find a mission in life the 'evil of dreaming' which had tortured her simply came to a stop.

Woman lives for man, we are told, her main interest in life is passion, and love is her whole existence. But the day-dreaming, the fantasies, soon stop if reality is allowed to come in.

Charlotte Brontë's characters positively threaten to explode with the frustration that disturbed and enraged Florence Nightingale. Jane Eyre 'longed for a power of vision' which would enable her to escape the prison of an isolated house and 'reach the busy world, regions full of life which I had heard of but never seen'. The character becomes a mouthpiece for her creator:

> It is vain to say human beings ought to be satisfied with tranquillity: they must have action; and they will make it if they cannot find it. Millions are condemned to a stiller doom than mine, and millions are in silent revolt against their lot. Nobody knows how many rebellions besides political rebellions ferment in the masses of life which people earth. Women are supposed to be very calm generally: but women feel just as men feel; they need exercise for their faculties, and a field for their efforts as much as their brothers do; they suffer from too rigid a constraint, too absolute a stagnation, precisely as men suffer; and it is narrow-minded in their more privileged fellow-creatures to say that they ought to confine themselves to making puddings and knitting stockings, to playing the piano and embroidering bags. It is thoughtless to condemn them, or laugh at them, if they seek to do more or learn more than custom has pronounced necessary for their sex.

It is true that grievance does not make for great art. *Wuthering Heights*, not only the finest English novel written by a woman, but quite simply the greatest English novel that anyone has produced, does not contain any overt protests or grievances, there is nothing to be read between the lines. It is all *in* the lines, one great burst of rage and passion, a case of total sublimation. When Catherine cries 'I am Heathcliff' it is also her creator speaking.

This is not to say, of course, that every woman writing in the nineteenth century was consciously or subconsciously at war with

the society in which she lived. By and large it is only the rarer
spirits at any given time who have a sharp sense of what is wrong
(though this does not necessarily mean that they feel themselves to
have been particularly wronged or express themselves, necessarily,
as aggrieved). George Eliot reacted to the feminine situation with
ironic comments, Charlotte Brontë with passionate anger. The
problem is dealt with most explicitly in *Shirley*, touched at more
rarely in *Jane Eyre*. Jane is a passionate fighter, even as a child. When
the saintly Helen tells her to be patient and forbearing, Jane
answers: 'If people were always kind and obedient to those who
are cruel and unjust, the wicked people would have it all their own
way: they would never feel afraid, and so they would never alter,
but would grow worse and worse. When we are struck at without
reason, we should strike back again very hard; I am sure we should
—so hard as to teach the person who struck us never to do it again.'
But Mrs. Henry Wood, for instance, largely unread today and
remembered as the author of popular bestsellers, subscribed to a
conformist view of society and morality, as popular bestsellers
usually do. The message of her books, the warnings and admoni-
tions contained in them are reminiscent of the messages hidden in
the love stories of the popular women's magazines today, and
reiterated at the back, amongst the letters of advice.

East Lynne was the most popular and entertaining of her many
novels, and in it we learn of the dreadful fate that awaits any woman
who, like Anna Karenina, leaves house and home for a lover:

How fared it with Lady Isabel? Just as it must be expected to fare,
and does fare, when a high-principled gentlewoman falls from her
pedestal. Never had she experienced a moment's calm, or peace, or
happiness, since the fatal night of quitting her home. She had taken
a blind leap in a moment of wild passion. . . . Oh, reader, believe me!
Lady—wife—mother! should you ever be tempted to abandon your
home, so will you wake. Whatever trials may be the lot of your
married life, though they may magnify themselves to your crushed
spirit as beyond the endurance of woman to bear, *resolve* to bear
them; fall down upon your knees and pray to be enabled to bear
them: pray for patience; pray for strength to resist the demon that
would urge you to escape; bear unto death, rather than forfeit your
fair name and your good conscience. . . .

The dangers for anyone who followed Lady Isabel's course, and left husband and children for a lover, were of course real enough. Lady Isabel, like Anna Karenina, not only faced social ostracism and the humiliation of the lover's fading passion, but the loss of home, financial security and children. Jane, on the other hand, passionately independent but just as bound by the morality of her own time, preserved her good name when she discovered that Rochester was committing bigamy by rushing out into the night, a pauper. One could side with the rebel Charlotte's heroine, who chose humiliation as schoolmistress and governess, proud on a tiny pittance per annum, or choose the path of safe, comfortable conformity that Mrs. Henry Wood advised, crushed spirit included. But by the middle of the nineteenth century one had to take sides: the cosy equanimity of Jane Austen, whose heroines always managed to combine sense and sensibility on their inevitable progress to the altar, had gone for good.

The evils and dangers of a woman thrown back on her own emotions have long been recognized by perceptive women. On the whole male commentators on womanhood, whether philosophers, psychologists, novelists or poets, have been content to say that women are more interested in love than men, that they are naturally more emotional and unstable, and leave it at that. But those women who have been unable to accept the *status quo* with regard to their own sex have understood both the cause and the danger. That the cause was a social set-up which focused all a woman's time and thoughts on making herself attractive to suitors and, later, to her husband; and the danger was that, too preoccupied with emotions, if only through lack of anything else to do, through boredom, as well as the fact that love was the mission in life assigned her by society, a woman became vulnerable to passion and might end up like Lady Isabel. 'Women ought to endeavour to purify their heart,' wrote Mary Wollstonecraft, 'but can they do so when their uncultivated understandings make them entirely dependent on their senses for employment and amusement, when no noble pursuits sets them above the little vanities of the day, or enables them to curb the wild emotions that agitate a reed, over which every passing breeze has power?' A woman who had been taught to spend all her time pleasing men would, once she was no longer able to please her husband, inevitably turn her charms on other males, concluded Mary Wollstonecraft. And she had no doubt that the power of charms must fade with familiarity. 'The woman who has only been taught to please will soon find that they cannot have much effect on her husband's heart when the summer is passed and gone. Will she then have sufficient native energy to look into herself for comfort, and cultivate her dormant faculties?' These words, published in 1792, show a far greater sense of sexual reality than the advice so often given to housebound wives in popular magazines today: smarten up before *he* comes home. If moral principles restrain a woman from infidelity, says Mary Wollstone-craft, she will become bitter and retreat into a private fantasy life instead. But the real basis of her objection to Rousseau's views on the education of women is that it makes them unfit for the very jobs that Rousseau assigns to them—the education of children and companionship to man. People who are constantly swayed by their emotions rather than ruled by reason are not good for chil-dren, and companionship between husbands and wives is impossible 'when their pursuits are so different'.

Both Charlotte Brontë and George Eliot understood that the confined life of woman as opposed to the active one of man made for a basic incompatibility in love and marriage which could prove disastrous. We see just how disastrous in *Middlemarch*, where a serious young man with ambition but no capital who, according to the custom of the time, should have postponed marriage, is trapped by the arch wiles of a young miss whose whole business in life was to make herself attractive. 'Poor Lydgate! or shall I say, poor Rosamond! Each lived in a world of which the other knew nothing.' Fit for nothing but extravagance and narcissism, Rosamond soon ruins her husband financially and is quite unable to understand his medical ambitions. Poor Lydgate is faced with the problem of 'bearing without bitterness . . . the blank unreflecting surface of her mind', and as the highly moral author of the *Vindication of the Rights of Women* foresaw, the woman who is taught to make the art of pleasing men her one function in life will not stop after marriage. Rosamond, wrote George Eliot, felt herself beginning to know a great deal of the world, especially in discovering . . . that women, even after marriage, might make conquests and enslave men . . . vanity, with a woman's whole mind and day to work in, can construct abundantly on slight hints. . . .

Charlotte Brontë is less detached and ironic, less capable of humour. In *Shirley* she gives us a young woman eating her heart out on the remote Yorkshire moors because she believes her love for Robert Moore, who runs a mill, is unrequited. Robert is always so busy and preoccupied (and with cause, it was the time of the Luddites and the mill was threatened). Here we have the unhappy Caroline watching him from a distance in church:

> By instinct Caroline knew, as she examined that clouded countenance, that his thoughts were running in no familiar or kindly channel; but that they were far away, not merely from her, but from all which she could comprehend, or in which she could sympathise. Nothing that they had ever talked of together was now in his mind: he was rapt from her by interests and responsibilities in which it was deemed such as she could have no part.
>
> Caroline meditated in her own way on the subject; speculated on his feelings, on his life, on his fears, on his fate; mused over the mystery of 'business,' tried to comprehend more about it than had ever been told her—to understand its perplexities, liabilities, duties, exactions; endeavoured to realise the state of mind of a 'man of business,' to enter it, feel what he would feel, aspire to what he would aspire to. Her earnest wish was to see things as they were, and not to be romantic. By dint of effort she contrived to get a glimpse of the light of truth here and there, and hoped that scant ray might suffice to guide her.
>
> 'Different, indeed,' she concluded, 'is Robert's mental condition to mine: I think only of him; he has no room, no leisure to think of me. The feeling called love is and has been for two years the predominant emotion of my heart; always there, always awake, always astir: quite other feelings absorb his reflections, and govern his faculties. . . .'

The endeavour not to be romantic was too much for Charlotte Brontë's heroines, they were passionately romantic. But they realized that hard work was the best antidote for frustrated love. Jane Eyre's humiliating position as an underpaid and despised governess was preferable to that of the girl who had no chance to work at all. Caroline and her friend Shirley Keeldar discuss the situation, the preoccupations that divide Caroline from Robert, the misery of waiting for him to return when he makes business trips to London, the fact that 'women have so few things to think about':

> 'Caroline,' demanded Miss Keeldar, abruptly, 'don't you wish you had a profession—a trade?'
> 'I wish it fifty times a day. As it is, I often wonder what I came into the world for. I long to have something absorbing and compulsory to fill my head and hands, and to occupy my thoughts.'
> 'Can labour alone make a human being happy?'
> 'No; but it can give varieties of pain, and prevent us from breaking our heart with a single tyrant master-torture. Besides, successful labour has its recompense; a vacant, weary, lonely, hopeless life has none.'

Most of Caroline's gloom is occasioned by the vision of herself as a lonely and useless old maid, should Robert not ask her to marry him. But he does ask her in the end. Rochester's mad wife dies and Jane can stop being a schoolmistress. Emotionally, Charlotte Brontë remained an old-fashioned romantic.

George Eliot was more realistic. In Dorothea she created a character who made a disastrous marriage with a hopeless old fuddy-duddy because she possessed a passionate and intelligent nature 'struggling in the bands of a narrow teaching, hemmed in by a social life which seemed nothing but a labyrinth of petty courses'. Because of her youth and lack of serious education Dorothea mistook Mr. Casaubon for a genius and attached herself to him as a sort of guiding light and father figure, hoping that her marriage would 'deliver her from her girlish subjection to her own ignorance'. Dorothea should have married Lydgate, one feels. She is the total opposite to the silly, flighty Rosamond, who reads light novels, plays the piano to charm gentleman visitors, and enjoys making herself pretty for parties. Dorothea, like Maggie Tulliver, wears dark, simple clothes, and her conversation is nothing if not serious. Securely wealthy, her earnest wish is to 'do good', and this is how she feels about her woman's world:

> . . . there was that stifling oppression of that gentlewoman's world, where everything was done for her and none asked for her aid— where the sense of connection with a manifold pregnant existence

had to be kept up painfully as an inward vision, instead of coming from without in claims that would have shaped her energies.—'What shall I do?' 'Whatever you please, my dear:' that had been her brief history since she had left off learning morning lessons and practising silly rhythms on the hated piano.

Unlike Charlotte Brontë, George Eliot circumscribes her characters. They are not her, she does not plunge herself into them, but the understanding and sympathy is unmistakable. When she writes of 'the sense of connection with a manifold pregnant existence' which Dorothea had to keep up 'painfully as an inward vision' it reminds us of Jane Eyre climbing up on the roof to look at the distant horizon and longing 'for a power of vision which might overpass that limit; which might reach the busy world, towns, regions full of life I had heard of but never seen'. Maggie Tulliver is also a victim of a circumscribed existence:

> she was as lonely in her trouble as if she had been the only girl in the civilised world of that day who had come out of her school-life with a soul untrained for inevitable struggles—with no other part of her inherited share in the hard-won treasures of thought, which generations of painful toil have laid up for the race of men, than shreds and patches of feeble literature and false history. . . .

and Maggie was destroyed. 'You are shutting yourself up in a narrow self-delusive fanaticism, which is only a way of escaping pain by starving into dullness all the higher powers of your nature,' Philip tells Maggie, and it was this fanaticism which made her refuse to marry Stephen and face social ostracism instead.

A real-life example of the difficulty, the ultimate impossibility of living one's life *through* a man, and finding one's whole *raison d'être* in the idea of love, is found in the early diaries of Tolstoy's wife. Later in life Countess Tolstoy was to become almost obsessionally busy: apart from going through thirteen pregnancies and raising the nine children who survived, she managed the estates, published her husband's works and copied and re-copied his writings. She wrote out *War and Peace* alone seven times, working at night with a magnifying glass to make out her husband's corrections. She also found time to make shirts for the family, play the piano and take and develop her own photographs. But she was married at eighteen, when Tolstoy was himself over thirty, a landowner and an established writer, and her early diaries reveal an attitude very different from the more practical jottings of her middle years.

> I can't find any occupation for myself. He is lucky to be so clever and talented. But I'm neither the one nor the other. One can't live on love alone; and I am so stupid that I can do nothing but think of him.[1]

In the previous entry she had written: 'I can hear him now, upstairs playing a duet with Olga. Poor Lyova! Always looking for amusements so as to be away from me.' This is the ultimate in narcissism, when a man playing the piano in his own home is, by implication, rejecting his wife. The wish constantly to attract, the constant need for a reaffirmation of love, must of necessity reach a blind alley, a point when reaffirmation is no longer possible. It is partly, of course, the result of a young girl's misunderstanding of the nature of sexual passion, but it is more than that. A girl's whole mission in life is to *be*, to attract, but she is not allowed to take the initiative in any way, she must sit and will for a response, dumbly, like some sort of motionless magnet. The result is an overwrought sensibility which, as Mary Wollstonecraft pointed out, is a danger and a nuisance not only to the woman herself but to those around her, particularly her husband. Right down to the present day a woman has to wait for the advances of a man, always uncertain, always on tenterhooks, never allowed to follow the dictates of her own mood in shaping relationships. The most progressive male would retreat in shock and alarm if a woman took the initiative.

'I have given my life to him,' complained the young Countess, 'I live *through* him, and I expect him to do the same.'

> . . . I love nothing and no one except Lyova. And yet one ought to have something else to love as well, just as Lyova loves his *work*, so that I could turn to it whenever he is cold to me. Such moments are bound to come more and more frequently; but in reality it has been like this all the time. I can see it quite clearly now, for I have nothing else to occupy my mind; he, of course, is too busy to notice all the details of our relationship.[2]

[1] *The Diary of Tolstoy's Wife* (translated by Alexander Werth), p. 87.
[2] Ibid., p. 98.

And later on we find her writing:

> Lyova has his work and his farming to think about, but there is
> nothing to keep my mind busy. . . . Much happiness and little work.
> And one grows tired even of the good things. One needs some work,
> if only as a matter of contrast. What was reverie and fancy ought now
> to become serious work—a *real* life, not merely a life of the imagina-
> tion.[1]

Add to this the debasement of sexual love, and you have the
whole picture. Thus Sofia both abhorred the physical act but
needed it as proof of her husband's love. At the same time it could
not be proof, since she spoke disparagingly throughout the later
diaries of the fact that her husband's reviving tenderness was only
sexual appetite, and nothing more. She more or less called him a
dirty old man. And yet, when Tolstoy was over eighty and their
sexual relations finally did come to a stop, she became hysterical,
unstable and jealous, and accused her husband of having a homosexual affair with the hated Chertkov. Matters were not helped by
Tolstoy's own debasement of physical love: as an elderly man he
preached total chastity whilst he was still making Sofia pregnant
with humiliating regularity. Incidentally, Tolstoy's motives for
debasing sexuality are the classic ones, mind always at war
with matter. In his early diaries he was constantly making rules
of conduct for himself, to be as regularly broken. One of them
read as follows: 'Regard feminine society as an inevitable evil of
social life, and, in so far as you can, avoid it. From whom, indeed,
do we learn voluptuousness, effeminacy, frivolity in everything, and
many another vice, if not from women? Who is responsible for the
fact that we lose such feelings inherent in us as courage, fortitude,
prudence, equity, and so forth, if not woman?'[2] This at the age of
nineteen. Nearly forty years later he noted: 'I have wondered why
so many intelligent and good men live so blindly and badly. The
reason lies in the power that women have over them. They let
themselves be carried along by the current because that is what
their wives or mistresses want. The whole story is told in bed.'[3]

---

[1] An entry made in 1891.
[2] *The Diaries of Leo Tolstoy (1847–52)* (translated by C. J. Hogarth & A. Sirnis).
[3] Note of 5th April 1885, quoted by Henri Troyat: *Tolstoy*.

The most amusing description of a female who would like to find a relief from boredom in an all-absorbing passion if only sex, and men in general, were not so vile, is, to my mind, one found in the diary of Fanny Burney. It derives its comic aspect from the eye of the beholder, the down-to-earth Miss Burney, who always found it possible to conform to her social surroundings without too much difficulty, even during those rather trying years at Court. In fact, who knows, perhaps the Miss W—— who confided her curious unhappiness to Miss Burney really did come to a sticky end:

> 'One thing', answered she, 'there is which I believe might make me happy, but for that I have no inclination: it is an amorous disposition; but that I do not possess. I can make myself no happiness by intrigue.'
> 'I hope not, indeed!' cried I, almost confounded by her extraordinary notions and speeches; 'but, surely, there are worthier subjects of happiness attainable!'
> 'No, I believe there are not, and the reason the men are happier than us, is because they are more sensual!'

Here the conversation was temporarily interrupted, to be continued later, with an admirable *finale* from Miss Burney:

> 'There may be, indeed, one moment of happiness, which must be the finding one worthy of exciting a passion which one should dare own to himself. That would, indeed, be a moment worth living for! But that can never happen—I am sure, not to me—the men are so low, so vicious, so worthless! No, there is not one such to be found!'
> What a strange girl! I could do little more than listen to her, from surprise at all she said.
> 'If, however,' she continued, 'I had your talents, I could, base as this world is, be happy in it. There is nothing, there is nobody I envy like you. With such resources as yours there can never be *ennui*; the mind may always be employed, and always be gay! Oh, if I could write as you write!'
> 'Try,' cried I, 'that is all that is wanting: try, and you will soon do much better things!'[1]

Many did try, and the result was a host of female novelists, born out of boredom, their ability channelled into one of the few courses open to them, a phenomenon which male commentators have been endeavouring to 'explain' ever since. 'Writing', said Florence

[1] 1780.

Nightingale when this occupation was suggested to her, 'is only a substitute for living.'

'This desire of being always women, is the very consciousness that degrades the sex,' wrote Mary Wollstonecraft, and time and again we find evidence in the writing of women which shows quite clearly that they understood the reasons for feminine neurosis and hysteria, and saw quite clearly the causes of over-emotionalism in their own sex. People are primarily human beings, and the desire to make them play ready-made male and female roles causes all the trouble. In 1848 George Sand wrote to Mazzini:

> I have seen your friend Eliza. . . . She is very kind, very intelligent, she must possess great qualities; but she is infatuated with herself. She has the vice of the day, and that vice no longer finds me tolerant as of yore. . . . *Man and woman* are everything to her, and the question of *sex*, in a sense at which the thought of man or woman should never exclusively stop, obliterates in her the idea of the *human being*, which is always the same being and ought never to perfect itself either as a man or as a woman, but as a soul and the child of God. That preoccupation produces in her a sort of hysterical state, for which she cannot account, but which exposes her to the designs of any scoundrel. I believe her conduct to be chaste, but her mind is not so, and that is, perhaps, worse. I should prefer her having lovers and never speaking about them, than having none and being constantly talking of lovers.[1]

The vice of the day: sex in the head, narcissism, hysteria, vulnerable to all male comers. Eliza equals Miss W——, and both have much in common with Anna Karenina, Madame Bovary and poor Lady Isabel.

Throughout history, said Freud, men (himself included) had knocked their heads against the riddle of femininity. True. But in saying that this did not apply to women, because they were themselves the problem, Freud was speaking only partial truth. They did not need to, because some of them, the more articulate and self-aware, already knew the answer. If arrogance had not made this impossible, he could have asked any woman for the answer.

[1] Letters of George Sand (translated and edited by Raphaël Ledos de Beaufort).

VIII

Today and Tomorrow

We live in a rapidly changing world, but I think it is often easy for literate people to exaggerate the extent of the actual changes that have taken place. One reads about test-tube babies, and one has already mentally scrapped the image of all the pregnant women from the world. Because a majority of the intelligentsia has dismissed religion we tend to forget that there is still a hangover of religious morality, and that a large majority of people still subscribe to religious ceremonial when it comes to birth, marriage and death. We read so much about 'the permissive society' nowadays that we tend to forget that, if society were really that permissive, no one would be writing or reading about it.

When I embarked on this book there was a good deal of debate as to whether the problems I was writing about were really relevant to the present day. 'You and I may have made mistakes, but the young generation now has everything sorted out.' I had my doubts. After all, I belonged to a generation already considered emancipated, so had my mother, for that matter. In fact my parents' generation belonged to one notorious for its permissiveness. All things are relative, of course, and sexual permissiveness is only one factor in the story. As far as the other factors were concerned, the fact that women do not always appear to make as much use of social and political freedom as they might is taken as proof of the fact that they are 'naturally' domesticated and uncompetitive, and prefer to concentrate on husband and home. To me it suggests that the emancipation is only superficial, that a few changes in the law, conceded only after long fights, cannot change old engrained attitudes overnight, or even over a generation or two. Habits are perpetuated in that bastion of social conservatism, the family. It would be foolish to suppose that we could change the social habits and prejudices of over two thousand years by passing a few bills. Sexual freedom does not necessarily imply psychological freedom, though it is a start. People talk as though the 'sexual revolution' was over, but to my mind it has hardly begun.

A child psychologist gave me a batch of school essays written, at his request, by girls of fourteen and fifteen attending a London grammar school. The year was 1968, and the set theme was 'Today is my eightieth birthday and I look back to the time when I left High School'. So, not just this 'young generation', but the one that is to follow; and moreover, girls of above average intelligence and with an urban background. Now, apart from one notable exception (a girl who said that her parents were divorced and that she thought marriage made people unhappy) the essays were monotonously similar. The great majority of the girls saw themselves married by the time they were twenty years old, and twenty-three (after a lengthy engagement) was the upper age limit for settling down. A year or two later all the young-marrieds had started a family of two or three children (almost all including a pair of twins). Although a lot of the girls contemplated some sort of further education, few of them visualized making use of their training for more than a year before marriage and a year or two after. Although some of the girls thought they would take a part-time job after the children started school, this was also regarded as a temporary arrangement— for some reason the girls thought they would become what they called 'an ordinary housewife' at the age of about forty-five. So the total aggregate of years worked, even after specialized training, tended to be at most only about ten years between the ages of fifteen and eighty! Just as marriage and honeymoon figured disproportionately large in the description of the early years, so the marriage of children and the arrival of grandchildren seemed the only reality in later years—not what they themselves could actually be doing. On the whole the girls who saw themselves as working for the longest period of time were those who wanted to become schoolteachers, and it is interesting to speculate how much this was due to the government's recent efforts to make up for the shortage of teachers by recruiting married women, and the publicity given to teaching as a 'suitable' profession for women even after marriage. 'Teaching hours suited both of us,' wrote one girl, 'as I was always back home before five o'clock to do the housework and cook a meal.' This was the kind of factor mentioned by several girls who had chosen teaching as a profession, particularly the fact that one could be home at the same time as one's school-age children. But none of these girls doubted that they would be doing housework. The year or two before marriage was the time for fun, travel and adventure. Real good fortune was being able to start married life in a home of one's own, instead of with parents or in-laws. One can argue about varying attitudes according to social background, but I think the variables tend to cancel each other out. The girls certainly came from a working-class area with no tradition of 'professional' mothers; on the other hand with a much longer tradition of two breadwinners in the family and the advantages this brings.

So these girls of tomorrow, the ones of above-average intelligence who will be making the most use of universities and training colleges, have their thoughts firmly fixed on marriage and motherhood. The focus on marriage and babies was very strong, and it was noticeable that after the birth of the children the future often became little more than a dim fog, with grandmotherhood at the end of it. What was also noticeable was the rather sad realism and lack of ambition: adolescent girls are supposed to indulge in fantasies and daydreams, but nearly all these girls seemed to plump for a drab sort of safety. Even the boys they married, the highlight of eighty years, were chosen because they were sensible and reliable. The one exception was a girl who saw herself as a film star, and married a film director called Sean. Marriage was followed by an avalanche of dramatic offers, but: 'I decided that this was the point at which I had to break away from Acting. I could not be a good wife and a good actress. I decided to take a few private pupils for Speech and Drama at our home. In that way I could choose my working hours so that I was not working when Sean was home. That was the wisest decision of my life. It saved my marriage.' So the exception turns out after all to prove the rule, the lesson has been duly handed down once more, that marriage is what counts for a woman, ambition is dangerous, and the wildest wings must be clipped. A basic assumption in all these essays, and one that is still made by our society as a whole, is that housework and the care of a man and of children is a woman's work and duty, that marriage is the most important factor in a woman's life, and that any other interests she may have must be curtailed by the demands that these duties make on her.

Although we have come some way since the Victorian age, it is not really that far, and the change has only been partial. No one doubts that at some stage a woman has to make a choice between her own ambition and her marriage, and in the eyes of society there is in fact only one choice to be made. A girl of fifteen knows both about the choice and what the answer is. It is not an issue that crops up in a boy or man's life, in fact marriage and the responsibilities of a family are regarded as a spur to ambition, since they give him social status and also cost money. A woman's career, particularly if it is successful, is often blamed for the break-up of a marriage, but never a man's, and if by some freakish chance a woman should earn more than her husband this is regarded as a danger to the relationship which warrants yards of printed advice—mostly that the woman should give up her job at once or conceal the dreadful fact with lies. The man's career is not taken into account in analysing the break-up of a marriage, because the man is regarded as the natural breadwinner. His job may take him away from home for nine months out of twelve, but no one would actually blame him for not changing it, and the fact would certainly not provide grounds for a divorce if his wife decided to sue for one.

The most conservative thinkers regard the lack of change as proof of the fact that women naturally prefer to play a traditional role, that the passive acquiescence evinced in these schoolgirl essays is biological. More liberal thinkers will concede that social conditioning has a lot to do with it, but fall back on the young child's need for security and love as a justification for continuing the *status quo*.

Now, no one would dispute that young children need love and security, but the assumption behind this argument is that there is only one way of giving these things to a child, and that way is considered the Freudian one. We have already analysed the patriarchal motives and attitudes behind Freud's psychology, and the present-day emphasis on the importance of marriage as a background for the young is really a continuation of the same thing, though the ground has shifted under masculine feet by now. Fifty years ago the Freudian would argue that a woman's rightful place was in the home and that if she tried to push her way into affairs that were none of her business this was evidence of her sense of inferiority, of penis-envy. Nowadays a woman with ambition is still accused of trying to compete with her husband, particularly if the marriage is not working too well, but the Freudian analysis of family life is mainly used to justify the perpetuation of marriage, not for the sake of the marriage partners themselves, but for the sake of the children. And the motive behind this argument is a dreadful suspicion that the father, once he is no longer the only breadwinner, may not be necessary at all. That he is, in fact, becoming redundant. This would mean the collapse of the whole patriarchal system. So, for instance, it is often argued that children who are not brought up within a conventional marriage, with a father and mother figure, are liable to become homosexuals or juvenile delinquents. This kind of argument ignores all the other factors which are liable to be present in a one-parent home or other aberration from the norm, given our present state of society. Nowadays abnormal homes are 'broken' homes, the situation is not usually one of choice. The poverty and deprivation that face a family once a father deserts his family can help to shape juvenile delinquents and adult criminals; the social deprivation, the emotional bitterness and frustration that result from the breaking of a conventional marriage contract can lead to parental domination as a form of emotional compensation which results in homosexual tendencies. From the way people defend the conventional two-parent household one would think that a child brought up solely by its mother or, for that matter, its father, would never clap eyes on anyone other than its parent, grow up as hermetically sealed from the realities of a heterosexual world as Miranda was. But the world is full of males and females—uncles, aunts, grandmothers, grandfathers, brothers and sisters, friends, lovers. A child automatically identifies with adults of its own sex. A boy spends as much time imitating admired football heroes as his own father. As for 'having to work through the Oedipal situation', a Freudian objection which is often raised, we—like Voltaire on having to live—do not see the necessity. But then we are not interested in authoritarian repression as a form of education.

I am not, of course, suggesting that it is not desirable or pleasant for a child to be brought up within a marriage of genuine love and harmony, if and when this is possible. But people's expectations of marriage have risen just as much as their expectations of a high living standard, and already many children are being presented with a succession of father images at five-year intervals, which is surely worse than no father image at all. All I am saying is that nowadays children are made the main justification, unnecessarily and I suspect insincerely, for the continuation of traditional family life and marriage. Children are made the excuse for cowardice, and also for misery and hypocrisy. And after all, the children of today are the adults of tomorrow, so what is a point of a cycle that merely repeats itself? Should you stay married for the sake of your children, just so that they in their turn should stay married for theirs? I reject the notion of one generation 'sacrificing' itself for the next generation, if that is really what people are doing, which is dubious. And, what is more, the next generation is far from grateful, does not condone the sacrifice but finds it an embarrassment. The children of broken homes certainly have their problems, but the fact that the children of homes artificially maintained often despise rather than respect their parents should tell us something. Adults who are not true to themselves can teach their children nothing.

At first glance it looks as though we are prophesying the return of the dreaded matriarchy, of a new race of women who merely use males for the purposes of pleasure and impregnation, a truly masculine nightmare where infants do not know how to look up to the father figure, do not even know what it means, and men do not know how to respect themselves. But in fact this is very far from being the case, if only because the importance of childbearing has decreased and will continue to diminish in the future. For this reason alone a radical change of attitude to the private and social role of women is needed. The old matriarchies may have had their fertility goddesses, but our preoccupation nowadays is with in-fertility. Private individuals practise birth control, both in marital and extra-marital relations, and governments worry about the population explosion, which is regarded as *the* most serious prob-lem of the century.

A hundred years ago it was normal for a married woman to give birth to ten children, nowadays the average is about two. The time may not be far off when no woman would be allowed to have more than two children, and she may be forbidden to have any at all for genetic reasons. And no doubt when the age of test-tube babies arrives pregnancy and parturition as we know it will be considered primitive and barbaric. But we do not have to look that far ahead, it is quite enough for us to look at the situation today.

It is not just that the years of childbearing have shrunk. Life expectancy has increased enormously. Three hundred years ago the average lifespan was just half what it is now; a hundred years ago the woman who survived ten childbirths could consider herself fortunate. The woman who has two children nowadays will, at most, be devoting seven full-time years of her life to them, if there is a two-year age-gap between them and both children start school at the age of five. That leaves an awful lot of adult living. About half a century, in fact. Is it wise or sensible to push those fifty years into the background, to create a situation where schoolgirls see that vast expanse of time as an unimportant miasma, simply for the sake of those important, harassing hectic years that look as though they will never end, but do, in fact, soon come to an end? Children who have been adequately brought up become independent very quickly, this is the purpose of education and upbringing. The clinging mother who is fighting off the idea of her own inevitable redundancy either retards the child's healthy development by re-fusing to allow him to become independent, or becomes an em-barrassing millstone for both husband and children, a cause of unnecessary guilt. Children do not ask to be brought into the world, and neither do they wish to repay an unasked-for sacrifice.

Old ideas and attitudes die hard, they are perpetuated through the very structure of family life, and one of the main hindrances to a really fundamental change of attitude is the institution of marriage itself. The fact that it still exists as an institution sanctified by the State as well as the Church shows that there has not been any very radical change of attitude with regard to men and women and their relationships to each other. I think that at the moment we are trying to ride two horses at once. We recognize the need for change, and at the same time we cling to old values, because we were brought up with them and we are not all that sure with what to replace them. This process of double-think is very obvious, for example, in the public attitude to abortion law. On the one hand we know that not only justice but practical common sense makes a more liberal abortion law essential, on the other hand we talk about child-murder and the sanctity of human life. One can argue till the cows come home about the ethics of not allowing a woman autonomy over what happens to her own body, but it is certainly hypocritical to take this line when one condones the prevention of conception. Where does murder begin? But the attitude which only condones sexual intercourse for the purpose of childbearing (particularly with regard to women) has still not quite died out. One still pays for one's mistakes, only the mistakes are rather more literal ones.

We are also trying to ride two horses with regard to marriage, and the increasingly frequent attempts at marriage reform also reveal muddled thinking: a recognition of the need for reform on the one hand, and a reluctance or inability to relinquish old concepts of behaviour which we regard as fundamental to our sense of values. We dare not be inconoclasts, we cannot relinquish the old gods because so much has been sacrificed to them. The idea of sacrifice is tolerable and even ennobling, but if a person becomes aware that the sacrifice may have been unnecessary, this is an awareness that cannot be borne and has to be shut out. Old soldiers are usually tremendously patriotic. So people who behave as their parents behaved before them, acting out a socially prescribed role because they dared not do anything else, will justify their conduct on moral grounds to their own offspring and thus help to perpetuate the old pattern of behaviour. For example, a middle-aged woman may be subconsciously aware that she has not made the most of her life, that she need never have devoted so many of her adult years to domestic occupations, but that it is too late to reverse the pattern: being unable to face this appalling fact she justifies her own existence by forcing her daughter into the same mould, by emphasizing the all-importance of marriage, by exaggerating the importance of household chores and making a mystique out of them. Or a man who lacks the courage to escape from a loveless relationship will justify his conduct on moral grounds. Unsatisfying, 'safe' work, the job done year after year with only a pension to look forward to can be justified in the same way.

The harsh fact of the matter is that the institution of marriage which we are now trying to reform so unsuccessfully is based, not on love, sentiment or compatibility, but on economic necessity. In the nineteenth century the pill was amply coated with sugar, but underneath it was bitter enough. More primitive marriages were based on partnership, on an association where the labour of both man and woman was needed. Middle- and upper-class marriage in the nineteenth century in Europe was basically the purchase of sexual favour in return for board and lodging. If the bargain, once struck, was harshly one-sided, this was due to the fact that a woman had little or no alternative. She was excluded from higher education and remunerative work, and she could do little or nothing to stop the steady stream of pregnancies once she did form an association with a man. So she had little choice but to place herself on the marriage market, display her charms in the hopes of catching the highest bidder, and hope for the best. She had to play the game by the rules, her virtue really was important, because her continuing livelihood depended upon it.

This is a concept of marriage which we do not recognize now. No doubt many people a hundred years ago thought that the sugar was in fact the pill. The idea of two people being tied together, not by love, but by economic necessity, is abhorrent to us. It smacks of prostitution. We feel that men and women should choose to marry each other for love, and that, on the whole, they should part if they no longer care for each other at all, if the marriage becomes a battleground. But at the same time we make this state of affairs very difficult to achieve because we still treat a man and his wife as an economic unit. A man's wife and children are still regarded as his financial dependants, and, because of the way we live, they usually are just that. Property is held in common, insurance and pensions and income are assessed in common, equal pay is postponed as an idealistic luxury. A belated realization that abandoned and dependent wives are placed in an intolerable position even today has led to attempts at legal reform which are so muddled that it is impossible to put them into effect. No doubt these attempts at reform will go on for some time, and none of them will make much difference, because they attack the symptoms and not the root cause. The truth of the matter is that one cannot afford to cultivate sentiments and at the same time maintain the institution of marriage. In the East it was only rich potentates who could afford a harem, in the West it is only millionaires who can really afford divorce, as long as economic dependence is part of marriage. We are democratic enough to think that fine feelings should be available to all, and we now pay legal aid so that anyone who has grounds for a divorce can get one. But only the rich can afford more than one dependent family, and there is no point in arguing about the share that an ex-wife should receive if there is nothing to share out. Our present difficulties with regard to marriage are largely due to the fact that we perpetuate a legal partnership based on finances, but allow people to contract in and out of it for reasons which have nothing to do with money.

This anomaly means that a lot of people are entering into legal contracts with no real understanding of what is involved. When, as most people do, they get married because they are in love, they become involved in a legal contract which, unless it is dissolved by a complicated process, is intended to be binding for life. A parson may enumerate your moral obligations during the wedding service, but a registrar does nothing to make you aware of your civic obligations. There is no printed contract to be signed, only a skimpy marriage certificate. When you consider the care with which people go over a five-year lease for a flat. . . . The very fact that fifteen-year-old girls today do not expect to work to support themselves for more than a couple of years proves that marriage is still considered as an economic unit. Unfortunately, our progressive ideas on human relationships, now being gradually condoned by the law, means that these girls are building their suburban dream houses on sand, being lulled into what may prove to be a very false sense of security. The educational choices that girls make in adolescence are all-important in this respect, and we know that the very young are also the very ignorant when it comes to human relationships. Divorces, falling out of love and such like, are things that happen to other people, not to oneself.

People are unwittingly hoodwinked into a situation, and no one is really to blame. The valuable lessons of experience are usually learned too late. The great social machine grinds creakingly on, swallowing us all up. Engineers try dabbing a little oil on here, tightening a screw there, when what is really wanted is a total overhaul. Attempts at a more liberal attitude to divorce, abolishing the idea of the guilty party and making it possible to obtain a divorce without mutual consent, have been vigorously opposed by women's organizations and by Members of Parliament as giving inadequate safeguards for the economic provision of a wife and her children. (Present divorce law also provides inadequate safeguards, so that a really determined woman will try to safeguard her interests by refusing to give her husband a divorce, or by feathering her nest first with the threat of refusal—hence the need for reform!) And they are right to oppose reform, just so long as a woman's economic welfare is inextricably tied up with marriage, and as long as there is not equal pay and opportunity, as long as a divorced woman does not even get an old age pension as the reward for her domestic labours. On the other hand, can you ever make young girls and women make real use of the opportunities that do exist, really make an issue of equal rights, until marriage actually appears less secure, until it looks, even to the most short-sighted, like a sentimental sham, providing about as much security as the exchange of gold rings over a village wishing well? So in order to get anywhere at all, a whole lot of reforms would have to come about simultaneously, and this is obviously asking too much of the overloaded machinery of government. It is also asking rather a lot of human beings, who do not take easily to radical change.

Either one goes on gradually liberalizing the divorce laws, until marriage stands exposed as a hollow sham in which no one would wish to engage, or one takes a short cut and abolishes marriage altogether. Either way women must be treated as total human beings in their own right, and not as appendages to a man. Either way children must be treated as primarily the responsibility of the state, since women will go on producing offspring and cannot be expected to face the economic burden alone. This means fairly substantial child allowances for all children, and sufficient state and/or industrial nurseries for children. It is time that the state stopped footing the legal bill for people to sort out their matrimonial wrangles in court and got down to realities, and the easiest way for this to happen would be for there to be no matrimonial rights or joint property to wrangle about. It is often argued that in fighting for the rights of mothers one tends to overlook the rights of fathers. On the whole, the fathers have themselves been to blame for this—in a patriarchal society they were all too easily able to take them for granted. But if the state were made economically responsible for the young there is no reason why the rights and, at the same time, responsibilities of the father should not be recognized through the income tax system. A man who paid tax to the state (then repaid to the mother in the form of a child allowance, unless the father or some other person had care of the child) would at the same time have his paternal rights officially recognized. Naturally there are going to be squabbles about access and custody if the couple have ceased to live together (and of course the lack of official marriage need not stop people having a joint *ménage* if they want to) but these also occur in divorce cases now, where it is normal for the wife to be paid a child allowance by the ex-husband, and she has custody while he has reasonable access to the child. There are fights now over access and custody, but usually it is not the child that the couple are fighting about, and on the whole most fathers are happy to leave care and custody of their children to the mother. There is no reason, of course, why this system should not be reversed, with the mother paying tax for a child which is cared for by the father. In fact I do not see why, in principle, both parents should not be taxable for their children. In practice, of course, the majority of women would not be paying the tax, since this liability would be offset by allowances to cover expenses involved in caring for the child.

I suppose it all sounds very complicated, unnecessarily so, perhaps, but the attempt to keep the institution of marriage and at the same time to make it easier to divorce is already proving a time-wasting and expensive burden to the law-courts, and the situation is bound to get worse. The divorce rate is rising and will inevitably continue to rise. Overworked courts now spend hours making maintenance orders, and many more hours trying—against hopeless odds—to keep them enforced. Separated wives, usually from the poorest sectors of the community, who rely on magistrates' courts, come off worst.[1] 'Because the majority of married couples do not have any property to squabble over in the law courts, they cannot even pay the lawyer, who is paid for by the state; all they have are hire purchase commitments and perhaps a heavily mortgaged house. Once these marriages break up officially (with the help of legal aid from the state) there is misery and poverty for the abandoned wife and children, and the state has to help as best it can. Punitive measures against these fathers are useless and simply cost more money. Surely a system whereby the state recognized its responsibilities to children as I have outlined above would be much more constructive and workable in the long run? It would certainly make for more human dignity. That human beings should be economically tied, willynilly, is neither dignified nor necessary. Essentially the days are past, and should be past, when a man had to buy sexual gratification by promising lifelong economic security. People all too readily forget that birth control has meant a sexual liberation for men as well as women! Under these circumstances women who think that being a wife alone gives them some kind of status, that condescending to give a man 'the best years of one's life' entitles one either to lifelong leisure and security or to lifelong devotion are a walking anachronism.

[1] See Appendix.

But as long as we have an institution as anachronistic as marriage I am afraid we shall go on having a large body of anachronistic women. In a world where free love is possible (by which I mean not promiscuity, but love without economic strings) I doubt whether most men, if they really thought about it, would want to continue the patriarchy with its concomitant institution of marriage. Why tie yourself for life to a woman when you can have her anyhow, why pay through the nose for what you can have free? What is wrong with allowing a woman equal pay if it means you do not have to support her? The fact that she may also compete for your job—and perhaps get it—must be faced. But in a non-patriarchal society where men are not competing for women by competing so strongly with each other (in order to prove themselves the best breadwinner, like male animals proving their physical strength) this would no longer be so damaging to male self-esteem. After all, a man's sense of his own masculinity is as false in a patriarchal society as a woman's sense of her own femininity. And women? Until marriage is either abolished completely or has become a hollow sham I am afraid that women are going to make far too little effort to improve their own position. Their laziness during this century has been a matter for smug male satisfaction. But it is perfectly natural for any young woman to look forward to the images of married bliss, to want to have a husband and children and a home of her own, and to accept this future as a delightful alternative to the dreary prospects of learning a trade and having to go to work every morning. Dreams of love are much more attractive than studying to pass examinations, and not only to the female sex, it just happens that men are not offered the choice of making love their whole existence. Even for the more mature woman marriage suddenly seems an attractive form of retirement once working has become too much of a routine or perhaps too difficult. All this has nothing to do with hormones or the menstrual cycle. Even the desire for children is more related to dissatisfactions with everyday life than with any maternal 'instinct'—it is simply that the care of children looks like an attractive alternative to the dreary business of earning a living, and of course, the less ambitious you are, the more dreary that business is liable to become, and ambition in girls is discouraged. It has been and still is discouraged because it is regarded as detrimental to the harmony of marriage, which depends on clearly understood male dominance.

So we are faced with a vicious circle, with an anachronistic institution perpetuating anachronistic attitudes. Perhaps it is asking too much to expect to abolish overnight an institution that has lasted for so long, and we must wait for its meaning to be gradually eroded away over the next fifty years. It just seems a waste of a lot of potential living. Although people will no doubt go on forming relationships which last a long time (and by a long time I mean five years, not fifty), relationships which will not necessarily be by any means exclusive ones. I am sure that legalized marriage must eventually become a hollow sham. We are well on the way to that situation now, and we know it. The reactionaries know it, and to prove it a few diehard Members of Parliament recently suggested that there should be two forms of marriage, one which could be ended by divorce and one which could not! It sounds absurd, but it is indicative of the fact that nowadays we are being patently insincere when we say 'till death us do part'.

Just as a man of moderate means cannot support more than one wife and family, so a country of moderate means cannot afford equal education for men and women if the women are not making full use of that education. This is another way in which we have failed to adapt to new ideas, in which we have tried to become more liberal whilst still holding on to old values. The system of first- and second-class labour works very well in South Africa, for instance, because the South African government spends almost no money on the education and social welfare of the African workers. But if they gave them the care and education accorded to our women and then used them as unskilled labour they would have serious financial difficulties (as well as an imminent revolution). Cheap labour which has had a lot of money invested in it becomes very expensive, wasteful labour. No doubt it is better for children to have educated mothers, but the limit beyond which higher female education becomes unnecessary in the home is soon reached, particularly in the twentieth century, when children start school at the age of five or even younger. (In the nineteenth century many women taught their children until the age of about nine, when they were sent away to school.) Today there are almost as many women in our colleges as men. Many of them will only make very limited use of their qualifications, and many of them choose courses which are attractive in themselves (like literature or fine art) simply because they are attractive and because they do not envisage having to earn a living for the rest of their lives. College, in fact, can become a modern alternative to a finishing school or to that stop-gap job between school and marriage. The Victorians thought that music, art, reading novels, anything to do with culture and good taste, were suitable occupations for young ladies who did not have to earn their own livings, and our educational expectations for girls have changed remarkably little. Sir John Newsom, quoted in our opening chapter, is a witness to that.

The educational expectations have not changed largely because marriage is still regarded as the real career for women. Few boys are naturally ambitious, but the necessity of earning a living is drummed into them at an early age. Most parents also go on to point out that a specialized education makes it easier to earn a comfortable living, and that the pleasures of art and music, for instance, have to be balanced with the greater remuneration likely from the study of engineering. This, together with the law of supply and demand, ensures that we have enough engineers and that only the very gifted or very determined stick to music or fine art. The fact that we have almost no women engineers and very few women lawyers or physicists results from the notion that, since her real career is going to be marriage, a woman might as well study the things she really enjoys, like the arts. And if she happens to have no particular talent and does have to earn her living for a year or two, well, she can always take a course in shorthand and typing. It is also the reason why women are so often content to go on doing the subordinate and ill-paid jobs—teaching and nursing, for instance, and why these essential jobs can continue to be so badly paid. Women do not regard their jobs as lifelong occupations, nor do they regard them, unless circumstances force them to, as a way of earning a living—men do that, women pay for the little

extras, like holidays and new furniture. As a result, when circumstances force a woman to become the principal breadwinner of a
family, she is rarely in a position to do so effectively, whatever her
educational level. It is a vicious circle: the concept of marriage
makes women unable to be really independent, and her inability to
be independent makes it necessary to try and protect her with
marriage. But a start has to be made somewhere, and I feel it should
be made on all fronts at once, otherwise there will be a lot of
casualties.

I have talked a lot about economic realities, not because I am
indifferent to the nature and quality of human emotions, on the
contrary. I have talked about these matters because I feel one
cannot separate states of mind from outer realities. Economic
independence may not be an absolute guarantee of emotional independence and stability, but it is certainly a necessary *a priori*. No
one can entirely legislate or educate away pain and suffering, but
it can certainly be minimized. The end of a marriage is usually so
much more traumatic than the end of a love affair because it
involves economic matters, and the bitterness between husbands
and wives who are separating is almost always occasioned by
money matters. If the parents fight over the children and involve
them in their disputes it is really money they are fighting about.
When a marriage founders a wife is risking not only the loss of a
lover and companion but her home and her whole way of life, and
subconsciously this makes her cling to a man she might otherwise
have rejected or released long ago. Love, said Byron, was woman's
whole existence, and society had seen to it that it was her whole
existence. Modern psychologists note that women are more childlike, more emotional and show a greater degree of dependence, and
the reason is still the same. We are all vulnerable to each other, but
women have been made particularly vulnerable emotionally,
because they are more vulnerable in other ways, and we do not need
psychologists to tell us this. We have all of us seen evidence of this,
in our everyday lives, amongst our friends, in ourselves if we are
women, in our women if we are men. Our literature bears witness
to it, so do the women's pages of newspapers and the advice
columns of women's magazines, so do our mental health clinics.

I think the remedy lies in our own hands, and it will be found in social change, not on the analyst's couch. The change is one that men should welcome as much as women, because female neurosis and dependence does not make the lives of men any happier either. Now and in the future patriarchal attitudes will benefit no one, least of all the men.

Appendix

Maintenance 'no use' to wives[1]

Maintenance for separated wives through magistrates courts should be replaced by 'fatherless family' allowances which the State had the right to recover from the father, Mr. Louis Blom-Cooper, director of the legal research unit at Bedford College, London, told a conference on fatherless families in Oxford yesterday.

The present system, as research from his unit showed, simply meant that the mother was better off on supplementary benefit.

The research, which is due to be published next year, found that there were arrears of maintenance in no less than 70 per cent of a sample of all orders in force at the beginning of 1966. This meant that the wives—drawn almost entirely from the poorest economic group—lived in financial uncertainty from week to week and many simply gave up and fell back on supplementary benefits.

Attempts to improve the situation had failed. In 1958 attachment of earnings was introduced to take money from the husband's pay. Over seven years the unit found only 1 per cent of orders was still alive after twelve months.

Magistrates courts were unable to enforce maintenance. They could not call on the police to help find defaulting husbands as these were civil cases. Only some justices' clerks thought that tracing husbands was part of their work; often it was left to the wife,

So the 60 per cent of wives who applied for maintenance orders and got them would be better off under supplementary benefit from the start.

[1] The *Guardian*, 24th September 1969.

A fatherless family allowance would not cost much more than was paid now. Abolition of the courts' work would bring savings and the State would be able to search out husbands to recover money from them. The State was bound to be paying out under the present system if the husband had formed a new family.

Acknowledgements

My thanks are due to Mr. Richard Lansdown for making available to me the schoolgirl essays discussed in the final chapter of this book.

I have acknowledged my sources in footnotes but in addition I should like to thank Victor Gollancz Ltd. for permission to quote from *Male and Female* by Margaret Mead; Sigmund Freud Copyrights Ltd., The Institute of Psycho-Analysis and The Hogarth Press Ltd. for permission to quote from Freud; Mrs. Katharine Jones and The Hogarth Press Ltd. for permission to quote from *The Life and Work of Sigmund Freud* by Ernest Jones; Routledge & Kegan Paul Ltd. for permission to quote from *Purity and Danger* by Mary Douglas; and Guardian Newspapers Ltd. for permission to reproduce the article 'Maintenance "no use" to wives'.

Bibliography

Camden, Carroll, *The Elizabethan Woman* (Elsevier Press, 1952)

Clark, Alice, *Working Life of Women in the Seventeenth Century* (Routledge, 1919)

Douglas, Mary, *Purity and Danger* (Routledge, 1966)

Friedan, Betty, *The Feminine Mystique* (Gollancz, 1963)

Gavron, Hannah, *The Captive Wife* (Routledge, 1966)

Kinsey, A. C., W. B. Pomeroy and C. E. Martin, *Sexual Behaviour in the Human Male* (Saunders, Philadelphia and London, 1948)

Kinsey, A. C., W. B. Pomeroy, C. E. Martin and P. H. Gebhard, *Sexual Behaviour in the Human Female* (Saunders, Philadelphia and London, 1953)

Maccoby, Eleanor E. (editor) *The Development of Sex Differences* (Standford Studies in Psychology, Tavistock Publications, 1967)

Malinowski, B., *The Sexual Life of Savages in North-Western Melanesia* (Routledge 1932)

Marcus, Steven, *The Other Victorians* (Weidenfeld, 1967)

Marcuse, Herbert, *Eros and Civilization* (Sphere Books, 1969)

Myrda, A., and Klein, V., *Women's Two Roles* (Routledge, 1968)

Reich, Wilhelm, *The Sexual Revolution* (Vision Press, 1961)

Rover, Constance, *Women's Suffrage and Party Politics in Britain 1866–1914* (Routledge, 1967)

Russell, Bertrand, *Marriage and Morals* (Allen and Unwin, 1929)

Stephens, Winifred, *Women of the French Revolution* (Chapman & Hall, 1922)

Sullerot, Evelyn, *Histoire et sociologie du travail feminin* (Gonthier, 1967)

Index

Index

Index

Storr, Anthony, 23, 24, 26
Strindberg, August, 24, 26, 77–8, 79, 122, 130
succubi, 43, 48, 55, 60

Third Reich, 121, 133–4
Tolstoy, Leo, 95, 107–8, 112, 121, 163–5; *Anna Karenina*, 158–9, 167
Tolstoy, Sofia, 163–5

vagina dentata, 48
Victoria, Queen of England, 153–4

Webb, Beatrice, 154
Weininger, Otto, 23, 121, 122, 130–3, 144
witchcraft, 44, 54, 58–65, 69
witches, 43, 45, 58, 69; witch-hunting, 74; witch trials, 59–65, 69
Wollstonecraft, Mary, 24, 102, 107, 159–60, 164, 167
Wood, Mrs. Henry, 158–9
Woolf, Virginia, 19, 152, 155
Wordsworth, William, 95–6